2-17-2018

TO
GUINEVERE

Lady Patriot

it's All TRUE !

Ted Lange

TED LANGE

3-17-2018

To GUINEVERE

IT'S ALL TRUE!

Order this book online at www.trafford.com
or email orders@trafford.com

Most Trafford titles are also available at major online book retailers.

Printed in the United States of America.

ISBN: 978-1-4907-1314-4 (sc)
ISBN: 978-1-4907-1316-8 (hc)
ISBN: 978-1-4907-1315-1 (e)

Library of Congress Control Number: 2013915432

Trafford rev. 09/11/2013

 PUBLISHING®   www.trafford.com

North America & international
toll-free: 1 888 232 4444 (USA & Canada)
fax: 812 355 4082

Dedicated to

Mel Stuart

And

Dick Anthony Williams

Thanks

To E. Jack Kaplan, who introduced me to the story

And

To Steve Keh, who believed in my storytelling

And

A special thanks to Don Guisinger, Kay Ley,
and my wife, Mary Lange.

Lady Patriot opened September 7, 2012 at the Hudson Theatre in Hollywood, California with the following cast:

VARINA DAVIS	Anne Johnstonbrown
ELIZABETH VAN LEW	Connie Ventress
JEFFERSON DAVIS	Gordon Goodman
MARY BOWSER	Chrystee Pharris
OLD ROBERT BROWN	Ted Lange
JUDAH P. BENJAMIN	Paul Messinger
MR. SLYDELL	Robert Pine

Director:	Ted Lange
Set Design:	Adam Hunter
Costume Design:	Mylette Nora
Lighting Design:	Steve Pope
Stage Manager:	Vanoy Burnough
Producers:	Steven Keh, Mary Lange

Lady Patriot opened July 29, 2013 at the HanesBrand Theatre in Winston/Salem, North Carolina, at the National Black Theatre Festival with the following cast:

VARINA DAVIS	Anne Johnstonbrown
ELIZABETH VAN LEW	Connie Ventress
JEFFERSON DAVIS	Gordon Goodman
MARY BOWSER	Chrystee Pharris
OLD ROBERT BROWN	Lou Beatty, Jr.
JUDAH P. BENJAMIN	Paul Messinger
MR. SLYDELL	Robert Pine

Director:	Ted Lange
Set Design:	Adam Hunter
Costume Design:	Mylette Nora
Wardrobe Master:	Wendell Carmichael
Lighting Design:	Steve Pope
Producer:	Mary Lange

The Setting

Act I

It is the start of the Civil War and Confederate President Jefferson Davis and his wife, Varina, have moved from Mississippi to the new capital of the confederacy, Richmond, Virginia. They are settling into their own white house and getting accustomed to the idea of war and what must be done to secure their future.

Act II

The War is winding down and things are looking bleak for a Confederate win. Optimism and options are fading fast and Southerners must consider how to survive a Union victory.

Author's Notes

A history teacher once told me that history is written by the victors and school textbooks are the product of these victors. My teacher implied that there may be more to the story than is traditionally represented. Thus began my love of history and the untold story.

My quest for untold history continued with my journey as an actor. I love to research the characters that I embody and find layers that I can add to my portrayal. Discovering little known facts about a time or era and looking for anecdotes that might provide a character with idiosyncratic options can lead an actor away from obvious choices. This provides the actor with an abundance of rich levels based on the character's history. The characterization avoids the cliché and becomes a real human being. When I decided to become a playwright, this passion for historical research became an integral part of my writing process. I feel compelled to tell the story less known . . . the history of those in the shadows of the victors.

Lady Patriot is the third play in my historical trilogy about the early history of our country. When I first heard about this story from my friend, Jack Kaplan, I was astounded. My high school history books never mentioned a slave who was a spy for the Union Army. Obviously, this is the kind of story that my history teacher alluded to all those years ago. And so began my research and *Lady Patriot* was born. I conducted internet searches, talked to experts, and read voluminous accounts of this era and gradually pieced together the fabric of this tale. It is the story of three lady patriots who lived during the Civil War, Mary Bowser, Elizabeth Van Lew, and Varina Davis.

Mary Bowser is a college educated black woman who put her life in jeopardy to fight for the Union and freedom for all black slaves. A patriot! Elizabeth Van Lew is a Southern aristocrat who also believed in freedom for the slaves and did not want to secede from the Union. A patriot! Lastly, Varina Davis is the wife of Jefferson Davis. She was entrenched in the slave mentality of the South, immune to its inhumanity, and believed that her husband was building a new country for the betterment of Southern society. A patriot! Based on their true stories, *Lady Patriot* reveals an intimate look into their prejudices and patriotism as it peels away traditional stereotypes prevalent in our history books.

Other little known facts emerged for me during the research of this play. Judah P. Benjamin, a Jew, was the right-hand man to President Jefferson Davis. Many Jewish Americans are astonished to learn a man of their heritage was a key influence during the Civil War. Old Roberts's character epitomizes how the house slaves learned to survive and navigate in the master's domain. Jefferson Davis was known to drink and smoke cigars with his house slave at the end of the day.

I have tried to be fair to all views and put the characters in the context of their time. There are words in this play that may be offensive to the reader, actor, or audience. It is a product of that time. A great disservice would ensue if I whitewashed the verbiage of the 1860's and avoided words because they are distasteful to our modern political correctness. The authenticity of the language is vital to the historical context of slavery. It should offend us and educate us in the atrocities that it encompassed so that we can learn from the evils of this degrading aspect of American history and demand a more equal society for all Americans.

For the process of staging the play, I have divided the stage into thirds. Stage right is the Van Lew Pantry/ Herb closet. It is later transformed into the Davis White House Kitchen. Center stage is the Davis White House State Room/ Dining Room. Stage left is the office of Jefferson Davis. The opening garden scene is played downstage of the Davis Office and State Room. Music is crucial to creating the historical ambiance of the times. The songs for the pre-show audience arrival represent the Southern attitudes of the time. *I'm a Good ol' Rebel* should be played after the pre-show announcements and right before the show begins.

From the germination of this story, I was compelled to examine this historical time and the little known characters that fought for their beliefs. I was compelled to write this play using drama and comedy to take these events and mold them into a cohesive story line that entertains and educates. *Lady Patriot* is based on a true story . . . these events happened . . . check my bibliography. I was compelled to tell this story that lies in the shadows and reveal what was hidden by the victors . . . only then can we come together as a melting pot and sup in splendor at the same table . . . free of lies and certain of the truth.

Lady Patriot Music

Pre-Show Music Starts at Half Hour

1. Dixie (3:02)
2. Confederate Song, Wearing of the Grey (3:02)
3. Confederate Song, Battle of Pea Ridge (3:57)
4. Swanee—Al Jolson Arrangement (1:54)
5. Confederate Song, The Battle Cry of Freedom (2:45)
6. Southern Soldier Boy (2:32)
7. Rose of Alabamy (2:35)
8. Mammy—Al Jolson Arrangement (2:03)
9. Richmond is a Hard Road to Travel (4:35)
10. Dixie (3:02)
11. Battle of Bull Run (2:40)

Pre-Show Announcements

As theatre goes dark:

12. I'm a Good Old Rebel (1:51)

Lady Patriot

Synopsis

The inner sanctum of Confederate President Jefferson Davis has been breached. Information is leaking to the enemy . . . who is the spy? No one is privy to this information except Jefferson's advisors and they are beyond repute. Based on a true story, *Lady Patriot* reveals an intimate look into the prejudices and patriotism of three ladies who lived during the Civil War, Varina Davis, Elizabeth Van Lew, and Mary Bowser. *Lady Patriot* combines Lange's signature comedy and drama as it peels away traditional stereotypes prevalent in the South during the Confederacy.

Cast of Characters

Varina Davis is the First Lady of the Confederacy. She is the epitome of Southern gentility. She is a woman of strong beliefs, but knows how to support her husband.

Elizabeth Van Lew is a Southern aristocrat. She is a Union sympathizer, but she must mask her true feelings by pretending to be eccentric. Crafty and smart, she uses any situation to her advantage.

Jefferson Davis is the President of the Confederacy. A soldier at heart, he is given the task of commanding the war and starting a new country. He is a leader, who actually wants to micro-manage all details. The war has easily distracted him from domestic duty.

Mary Bowser is a college educated black woman. She must pretend to be an ignorant slave while she performs her duties in the Jefferson household.

Old Robert Brown is a house slave and an old hand at dealing with white masters. He knows how to work a situation so that he profits. He is past his prime and has given up the fight. He is an old dog that can not learn a new trick.

Judah P. Benjamin is a Jewish lawyer with a brilliant mind and knows how to deal with gentiles. He comes armed with charm, intelligence, and a way of making others feel comfortable.

Mr. Slydell is a Yankee journalist. He works for Horace Greely and the New York Tribune. He is an abolitionist and is soured by the Civil War he has to cover.

ACT I

Scene I

Richmond, VA. Jefferson Davis's White House Garden, July 1861. Varina Davis, Jefferson's wife, is a southern white lady who is 5 months pregnant. She is sitting on a small stool, fanning herself. Elizabeth Van Lew, a southern white lady, is digging up herbs and plants and putting them into a basket.

VARINA

What is that?

ELIZABETH

That's not it.

VARINA

But what is it?

ELIZABETH

I dunno . . . let me see. You know what that is?

VARINA

No.

ELIZABETH

Me neither . . . but whatever it is . . . it's rotten. Come spring, you need to re-plant this garden or otherwise you should send your gardener to a place where he will never hear the dogs bark.

                    VARINA

So much work to be done.

                    ELIZABETH

Don't worry, Varina, I'll help. You need help, I'll
help. That's what friends are for or why would you
call yourself a friend. Right? Right.

                    VARINA

Lizzy, I'm just plain overwhelmed.

                    ELIZABETH

First priority is the baby. Everything else will work
itself out.

                    VARINA

I hope so. Jeff has got so much on his mind. I just
don't want to be a burden. Everything in the house
is my responsibility . . . It just seems . . . well . . .
you know . . . I just think I got pregnant at the
wrong time.

                    ELIZABETH

Children come into this world when they need to
come. We don't really have a say. If you don't know
that, you're dumb as a bucket of rocks.

                    VARINA

Child's coming, right smack dab in the middle of a
war.

ELIZABETH
Where are your slaves?

VARINA
Most of my niggers are still in Mississippi. It'll be weeks before we get everyone here, moved in and organized. I don't know whether to scratch my watch or wind my butt.

ELIZABETH
Varina, I could lend you one of my girls . . . if you want. Just for a few days.

VARINA
Oh, Lizzy, that would be wonderful! I'm not moving as quickly as I like. This is my fifth child. It should get easier . . . but it doesn't.

ELIZABETH
My girl, Mary, can help you around the house. She's good in the kitchen . . . knows her herbs, cooks like an angel, and she is a hard worker.

VARINA
She doesn't break dishes?

ELIZABETH
Not even when she's mad.

Both women laugh.

VARINA

I'll take her.

ELIZABETH

Just for a few days. I need her back.

VARINA

Two weeks. Lizzy, just let me have her for two weeks, and I promise to give her back. What's that?

ELIZABETH

Used to be ginger. But it's all dried up.

VARINA

Lizzy, this is one pathetic garden.

ELIZABETH

Let's replant it now. You and I could do it.

VARINA

That's crazy Lizzy. We are out of season.

ELIZABETH

Plants don't care. Let's dig this garden up right now, me and you.

VARINA

Lizzy, I'm not digging up this garden. Don't be foolish. That's why we have niggers.

ELIZABETH

Okay, okay, okay, okay, okay. I've got some herbs at home. Okay, okay, okay, okay, I'll share.

Jefferson Davis enters.

JEFFERSON

A beautiful day for picking flowers, ladies.

VARINA

. . . and herbs.

Jefferson gives her a peck on the lips. He nods at Elizabeth.

JEFFERSON

Miss Elizabeth, how are you today?

ELIZABETH

I'm just a cracker looking for a barrel. How are you doing today, President Davis?

JEFFERSON

Don't you start with me, young lady . . . no formalities.

ELIZABETH

President Davis, if we are gong to build a new nation we must have structure. I'm sure that Lincoln's friends call him President Lincoln. You deserve no less respect than that Yankee.

JEFFERSON

Aren't you the civic-minded one? Okay Miss
Elizabeth, I accept your appellation and I will try
and live up to all that it engenders.

ELIZABETH

Thank you, President Davis. Well I must be going.
I will make sure I get those herbs to you Varina.
That is the first thing I must do, then mix the rest of
the day with my don'ts till I am somewhere in the
middle.

VARINA

Don't forget your nigger Mary and I will send Old
Robert round to pick her up.

ELIZABETH

I'll look for his arrival. Good day . . . good day . . . .
good day!

Elizabeth exits.

JEFFERSON

Are you going to give me another son, Varina?

VARINA

If the Lord sees fit, he will bless us with a healthy
son or a healthy daughter?

JEFFERSON

You are right. The health of the baby is the most important thing. I just think little Joseph would want a brother to play with.

VARINA

Then let us keep that thought in our prayers.

Jefferson kisses Varina.

JEFFERSON

Your hair looks beautiful in this Virginia sun

VARINA

You are certainly in a jovial mood.

JEFFERSON

I am married to the most beautiful woman in the South and I just got word that we won the battle at Bull Run. Whipped us some Yankee behind. Our boys were victorious. Who shall we name him after?

VARINA

My daddy of course.

JEFFERSON

That's fair . . . and if it's a girl?

VARINA

Why Mister Davis, she's gonna carry my name.

He laughs.

> JEFFERSON
> You delight me Varina. These are dark times and you can actually make me smile.

> VARINA
> Just doing my wifely duties . . . which is why I am here in our garden.

> JEFFERSON
> And what was 'Crazy Bet' doing in our garden?

> VARINA
> Jefferson Davis, don't you dare call her that!

> JEFFERSON
> Varina, honey, everyone in Richmond knows that woman is nuttier than a squirrel turd.

> VARINA
> Well, she did want to replant this garden, but crazy or not she has been very helpful to me. She's gonna loan me one of her niggers till the rest of ours arrive. I think that is a sweet thing for her to do.

> JEFFERSON
> You get no argument from me. As long as her nigger ain't crazy like her.

Varina suddenly grabs his arm, and starts to drop. Jefferson catches her.

VARINA
Jeff.!! Oh, Jeff, help me. Help me.

JEFFERSON
Varina, are you all right?

Varina holds on to his arm trying to catch her breath. She grabs her stomach.

VARINA
Lord have mercy. This isn't going to be an easy birth.

JEFFERSON
Come, let's go inside so you can lay down.

She tries to force herself to smile. Her husband helps her up . . . as the lights fade to black.

Scene II

Van Lew Plantation Pantry. Elizabeth is putting some bottles into a wooden box. She is being helped by a young black slave girl, Mary Bowser. The box is being held by an older black slave, Old Robert. Mary puts an item in the box.

ELIZABETH (in a harsh voice)
No, no, no, no Mary! Don't be stupid. I said red raspberry leaf tea.

Elizabeth takes the item out of the wooden box and gets the correct item and places it in the box.

ELIZABETH
See that? That is this one.

MARY
Yes, 'em.

ELIZABETH
Now get me three of those ginger roots over there.

Mary picks out three ginger roots.

ELIZABETH
No, Mary! The biggest ones we've got. Those won't last a week. Find me nice big fat roots.

Mary goes through the roots again and picks out some bigger roots.

MARY

Yes, 'em.

ELIZABETH

Varina's not having an easy pregnancy. These roots
will come in handy. Settle her stomach and take the
swelling out of her ankles.

MARY

Yes, 'em.

ELIZABETH

You remember how I told you to prepare them?

MARY

Yes, 'em.

ELIZABETH

Sambo . . . you let me know if Varina complains
about Mary. I'll send over another slave.

OLD ROBERT

Yes, Miss Elisabeth.

MARY

His name is Old Robert, Miss Elizabeth.

ELIZABETH

That's what I said.

MARY

No ma'am . . . you said Sambo.

ELIZABETH

Old Robert, Young Robert, Black Robert, Brown Robert, what difference does it make. He knows what I mean . . . don't you Sambo? You know what I mean. He ain't no fool Mary . . . he just a slave. Sambo, don't you know what I mean?

OLD ROBERT

Yes, ma'am.

MARY

You said it again.

ELIZABETH

Said what?

MARY

Nothing.

ELIZABETH

Something on your mind Mary B.

MARY

No ma'am.

ELIZABETH

Damn right. Mess with me. I'll make you feel lower than a toad in a dry well. Watch her you old coon, she can get feisty. I hear any complaints about your work Mary Bowser . . . even a whisper . . . you're coming home. You understand, me?

MARY
I'll be good. I promise.

ELIZABETH
Don't be making no promises you can't keep. Remember you represent me and the Van Lew family. I don't want you bringing shame on the name of Van Lew . . . even though that ain't your name. You are a Bowser straight up and down. That ain't no lie. Are you a Van Lew?

MARY
No ma'am.

ELIZABETH
Damn right you ain't. I told Varina you were a hard worker. Varina lost two children. Here, take the olive oil and you be sure to rub it on her stomach every evening.

MARY
Miss Elisabeth, you know I'm the best midwife this side of Richmond.

ELIZABETH
We got to get to the birthin' day, Mary B . . . for you to be her midwife. Now I don't want Varina lifting

anything heavy or staying up too late. It's your job
to make sure she is comfortable. You are only going
to be there for a little while. You may not even see
birthin' day.

MARY

Yes 'em.

ELIZABETH

Tarbaby, you heard what I told Mary?

OLD ROBERT

Yes, Miss Elisabeth.

ELIZABETH

I'm gonna stop bye next week to make sure nobody
pisst in the punch.

MARY

I promise you Miss Elizabeth, I'll keep Miss Varina
comfortable. She ain't gonna want for nothin'. I
knows my duty, and I knows how to do my duty.
I done already birth fourteen souls into this world.
Mostly white . . . ready to bring in more.

ELIZABETH

Not worried about you birthin' the baby, Mary
Bowser. Witch hazel's in this bottle. It's just that
Varina is a fragile woman. Her husband's gonna be
busy with the war. I know him . . . he ain't gonna
have time to look after his wife. You're gonna have

to do that. Hey, you old darky . . . you hear what I'm saying?

OLD ROBERT

Yes 'em.

ELIZABETH

Good. Take this box to the wagon.

Old Robert exits with the box.

OLD ROBERT

Yes, ma'am.

ELIZABETH (calls after him)

Don't drop the box or crack the bottles.

In a softer tone to Mary, almost a whisper

Good luck Mary.

She hugs Mary. Mary exits.

Black Out.

Scene III

Davis White House State Room. Jefferson and Varina are sitting at a table. Jefferson is writing a letter and drinking whiskey. Varina plays solitaire as she sips a glass of absinth.

JEFFERSON

How's the absinth?

VARINA

You know I love the green fairy. How's that Kentucky brew?

JEFFERSON

Good. Come here and let me touch your belly.

VARINA

Why?

JEFFERSON

Want to see if this child is gonna be special. Want to know whose bloodline is running strong through his veins . . . Howell . . . or Davis?

Varina crosses to Jefferson and he puts his hands on her stomach.

VARINA

I love your touch.

JEFFERSON

Oh yes . . . he got the Davis magic. This boy's gonna
be real special.

VARINA

Just like his daddy.

JEFFERSON

This child is gonna raise twenty kinds of hell and
leave his footprint where they say it can't be done.

VARINA

Just like his daddy.

Varina glances at the letter on the desk that Jefferson was
writing.

JEFFERSON

Varina, I think come September . . . I'm going to
appoint Judah Benjamin as my Secretary of War.

VARINA

The Jew?

JEFFERSON

He's a good man.

VARINA

He's still a Jew.

JEFFERSON

I like the lucidity of his intellect, he's loyal and decisive. Judah has a great capacity for labor.

VARINA

Jeff, you know plenty of Christians who could handle that post. Can't you give someone less . . . well, you know less . . .

JEFFERSON

Varina, you handle the house. I'll handle the war.

Jefferson gets up and exits.

VARINA

I'm so mad I could spit.

Black Out.

Scene IV

Davis White House Kitchen. Mary is preparing to bake some bread. She kneads the dough and flours the chopping block as she is preparing the bread. Old Robert enters with a tray of silverware. He starts cleaning the silverware.

MARY

I notice they run y'all ragged in them meetings. You need help?

OLD ROBERT

That's flour from my sack. No, little Mary, I'm fine.

MARY

Don't be afraid to ask. I'm a girl, but I'm young and I'm handy.

OLD ROBERT

I can see dat. I ain't blind, I'm just old.

MARY

Just thought I'd ask, that's all. I am of a mind that we should help one another, whenever we can. Who is the man with all the papers that keeps visiting Master Jeff?

OLD ROBERT

Dat is Mister Judah.

MARY

What he do?

OLD ROBERT

He the Confederate Attorney General.

MARY

What's that?

OLD ROBERT

Someone to smoke cigars with. The other cabinet members call him, 'The Shylock of the Confederacy.'

MARY

What's the Shylock?

OLD ROBERT

Damned if I know, but I don't think it's good.

MARY

Why do you say that?

OLD ROBERT

Just the way they say it . . . 'The Shylock.' How ya'll skills at brewing coffee?

MARY

Once a white man tells me how he likes it . . . he don't have to repeat it. And he can count on it being served that way every time.

OLD ROBERT

Little Mary, you full of yo self.

MARY

Got good reason to be.

OLD ROBERT

Oh.

MARY

Yes suh . . . I'm the best.

OLD ROBERT

No, you think you're de best.

MARY

I can hold three plates on one arm, and pour honey wine from a gallon pitcher with the other. I can pluck a chicken clean after wringing his neck and never miss a feather, flour him, fry him, and make sure the inside is juicy and the out side is crispy. I can set a table for twelve, put the big forks and the little forks in the right place, and make sure the food gets to the table hot.

OLD ROBERT

You can do all dat, can ya?

MARY

Oh yes, I can. I'm valuable. I ain't no ordinary nigger, Old Robert. I'm a special nigger. I know I don't look it . . . but I am. I know it and someday you gonna know it, too. You just tell me the day you want to educate yourself on the skills of Mary Bowser.

OLD ROBERT

We gwine see. Tell you what . . . I want you to brew me two cups of coffee. One is cream, no sugar. I want dat cup the color of Sarah Mae. De second cup I want black with one and a half spoons of sugar. Dat's for Massa Jeff. Now, he ain't gonna taste it . . . I is.

MARY

You is . . . ? Well ain't you the one.

OLD ROBERT

If'n it tastes like two spoons of sugar, don't come asking me if I need help. If'n it tastes like one spoon of sugar, don't come bragging to me, 'bout how special you is. If'n it tastes like I asked for . . . maybe, and dis here is just a maybe . . . maybe I might let you help me. Cuz, I don't believe in no special niggers.

MARY

You don't.

OLD ROBERT

Waitin' to find one.

MARY

What you believe in?

OLD ROBERT

I believe in special white folks. I know you ain't white so . . . gwine wait and see if you de other. Dese white folks you dealing with here is somethin' different.

MARY

You think they gonna win this war?

OLD ROBERT

I know dey gwine to win this war.

MARY

Maybe not.

OLD ROBERT

Don't fool yourself little Mary. Yankee talking about dese folks changing their way of life? You think dis white man gwine give up somethin' he love? You think dey gwine take dat kind of talk laying down. No sir. Dey gwine fight cause dey believe dey right. Ain't nothin' worse than fighting with a man knows he's right and think he got Jesus on his side.

MARY

I wouldn't under estimate those Yankees.

OLD ROBERT

Looka here, dese white crackers are some cruel sons of bitches. Seen what dey do when dey mad and seen what dey do when dey just sorta angry. Seen dem pretend to be Christian and seen dem pretend to be genteel. Dey would rather quit the U.S. of A., den give up dey slaves.

MARY

I don't think they gonna win this war. Federal government is too powerful.

OLD ROBERT

Dey already winning de war . . . and Lord help de child dey find out ain't for dem. Little Mary, heed my words . . . I can see what you want to happen. Keep dem thoughts to yourself. Dis here war ain't gwine free one nigger. Ain't gwine bring dese white folks back into de fold. Make sure you protect yourself. So dat you can survive which ever way dis wind blows.

MARY

Thanks Old Robert.

OLD ROBERT

Now let me see you brew two cups of coffee.

Black Out.

Scene *V*

Davis White House Office. Jefferson Davis and Judah P. Benjamin are looking at some maps.

JEFFERSON

How's Natalie?

JUDAH

She's good. Gonna be harder for me to get those bottles of wine, now that we are at war.

JEFFERSON

Damn if those French don't make a fine tasting wine. She been in Paris how long, now?

JUDAH

Fourteen years.

JEFFERSON

Fourteen years. How can you stand to be away from your wife for such long periods of time?

JUDAH

I see her every summer. She understands my work is here. We're soul mates so I don't think about it much.

JEFFERSON

I believe there is only one soul given to another soul. I lost the soul that was the love of my life. Back in '35. Married her in June, lost her to malaria in September.

JUDAH

Sarah Taylor?

JEFFERSON

Called her, Knox. Oh Judah, what a lady she was. That bastard . . . her father did everything he could to stop true love. Didn't want his daughter marrying a soldier. Loved that woman so much I stopped soldiering.

JUDAH

What did her daddy say then?

JEFFERSON

Said it didn't matter. I had soldiering in my heart. Truth is I had Knox in my heart.

JUDAH

Varina seems to be the perfect wife.

JEFFERSON

She's a beautiful woman, Judah . . . but you can not substitute beauty for passion. Varina's a good woman with strong opinions . . . but she ain't Knox.

JUDAH

J.D. she loves you.

JEFFERSON

True, fortune has smiled down on me in that regard . . . but, what is a marriage without the sweet tides of thoughts taking charge of your actions? Sometimes in the oddest moments, Knox will appear in my mind. What would she think of this? How would we share that adventure together?

JUDAH

It is a dilemma . . . but Knox is gone. Natalie and I never shared work in the same way you and Knox did. I like to keep my private life out of that arena.

JEFFERSON

Not to be dwelt on. Which reminds me . . . ah, Judah, next time you see Varina, I need you to charm her.

JUDAH

Charm her. Me? I hardly see her . . . and when I do she is very aloof. I can count the time on my left hand that we have even had a conversation.

JEFFERSON

We are building a new country, Judah. Politics seeps into the domestic as well as the political side of our obstacles. The ancient memories of my lovesick youth must be set aside. We must now solve the problems at hand. Be nice to her.

JUDAH

J.D., whatever I can do . . .

JEFFERSON

You are a gentleman, sir.

Black Out.

Scene VI

Davis White House State Room. Mary helps Elizabeth with her coat. There is a basket on the table. Varina enters with a mason jar of peach preserves and sipping absinth.

MARY
Baked you two loafs this time Miss Elizabeth.

ELIZABETH
What are you drinking Varina?

Mary exits with Elizabeth's coat.

VARINA
The green fairy.

ELIZABETH
Absinth is not good for the baby. You should try 'bitters'. It will settle your stomach.

VARINA
I like the taste.

ELIZABETH
I like the taste of Kentucky bourbon, but I know better than to drink it when I'm pregnant. Send Old Sambo by my place and I will give you my bottle of 'bitters'.

VARINA

Aren't you the sweet one.

ELIZABETH

We want you to have a healthy baby.

VARINA

My nigger Sarah Mae made these peach preserves. Add this to your basket.

Varina hands the jar to Elizabeth.

VARINA

This is my way of thanking you for the use of your nigger. Lizzy, she has been indispensable.

ELIZABETH

I knew you would like her.

Mary returns with two loafs of bread.

VARINA

She keeps my bedroom clean and orderly. She has done wonders for my feet and knows so much about keeping my stomach at ease. When I need her to play with my little Maggie, she knows just how to keep her occupied. Without even asking she keeps Jeff's office immaculate, dusting and washing the floors. I couldn't be more satisfied.

ELIZABETH

Mary, makes me proud.

MARY

Thank you Miss Elizabeth.

VARINA

Lizzy, I know we agreed that I would only keep her for a couple of weeks . . . but may I impose on your generosity for a little while longer?

ELIZABETH

Tell you what Varina . . . keep Mary till the baby comes.

VARINA

You don't mind?

ELIZABETH

Right now I need Mary less and less. My mother and I have been visiting Libby prison. We've been administering aid to the prisoners of war . . . caring for the sick. I know they are union soldiers, but it's only the Christian thing to do.

VARINA

I don't think I could tend a Yankee.

ELIZABETH

I just hate seeing those young boys treated badly. They are our enemies, but we Southerners are still civilized. You know we got the grandson of Paul Revere locked up in our prison.

VARINA

Guess he chose the wrong side.

Elizabeth puts the loaves of bread in her basket.

ELIZABETH

I would only ask one favor of you Varina . . . that Mary continues to bake this tasty bread for me. You can do that can't you Mary?

MARY

Yes ma'am. I think y'all will find these two loafs really delicious.

ELIZABETH

It's my weakness. God help me but every Monday morning I feel I have a right to give into my weakness.

VARINA

My weakness isn't bread . . . but every Monday morning I find myself giving into my own weakness. That is why my belly is in this condition today.

ELIZABETH

Until I find the right man . . . I'm going to have to settle on my breakfast toast. I look forward to a good hearty meal. Must be going. Send that old coon around for the bitters.

VARINA
Lizzy, you've got a true Christian heart. May God bless you.

Elizabeth starts to leave as Old Robert shows Judah into the sitting room. Old Robert carries a bottle of olive oil and a towel.

ELIZABETH
Old Sambo speak of the devil and up you pop. You come by my place and retrieve a bottle of *"bitters"* for your mistress.

OLD ROBERT
Yes, ma'am.

JUDAH
I'm early?

ELIZABETH
Yes, you are. Just like a Jew.

VARINA
Jeff will be back shortly. Old Robert I want you to go with Lizzy.

OLD ROBERT
Yes 'um.

Old Robert gives the olive oil and towel to Mary and leaves with Elizabeth. Judah crosses to Varina and kisses her hand.

JUDAH
How are you feeling today?

VARINA
My ankles swell.

JUDAH
Looks like you are going to have a healthy baby.

VARINA
Mary swears it's gonna be a boy.

MARY
Yes ma'am. That's how you carrying him.

JUDAH
A boy. Good news . . . another son to carry on the Davis name.

VARINA
He'll be William Howell Davis.

Mary exits.

JUDAH
A fine strong name.

VARINA

William Howell was my daddy's name.

JUDAH

Your son will be able to trace his roots. He will know from where he comes as he helps to build our new country.

VARINA

Our?

JUDAH

Mrs. Davis, you are not fond of me are you?

VARINA

Mr. Benjamin, I don't think about you one way or another. You are a colleague of my husband. He thinks you are valuable to the war effort. I'm a lady. I don't mix into the affairs of state.

JUDAH

You are not just any lady. You are the first lady of the Confederate states.

Does my being a Jew bother you?

VARINA

No.

JUDAH

Not at all?

VARINA

Not in the least . . . however the fact that you killed
our Lord and Savior Jesus Christ . . . does give me
pause.

JUDAH

Mrs. Davis, I am fifty years old. He died long before
I was born.

VARINA

I mean your people.

JUDAH

I was born in the West Indies, St Croix.

VARINA

You are a Jew. You know what I mean. You're
twisting my words.

JUDAH

No, Mrs. Davis, I am not twisting your words . . .
but I understand how you feel. There are many
Southern Christians that feel as you do. Usually
those that feel animosity toward me and my heritage
know very little of my faith.

VARINA

Did not the Jews kill Jesus Christ?

JUDAH

Actually the Romans did, Herod to be exact. Are you mad at the Catholics that are descendants from those Romans?

VARINA

Ain't to happy with Catholics either . . . but it was the Jews that betrayed Jesus.

JUDAH

Not all Jews.

VARINA

Most of them.

JUDAH

Mrs. Davis, do you think Jesus was mad at most Jews as he hung on the cross?

VARINA

I don't know.

JUDAH

He asked his father to forgive them. Mrs. Davis, America was founded on religious tolerance. I hope to have that same tolerance in the confederacy. Can you forgive me as Jesus forgave my brethren?

VARINA

(beat) I guess so.

JUDAH

Equality for everyone. Let us be free to worship our
faith. Jesus was a Jew. You love Jesus don't you?

VARINA

Of course I do.

JUDAH

I'm not asking you to think of me as Jesus, although
I sometimes feel unjustly crucified, but he did have
twelve disciples. All Jews . . . think of me as one of
the twelve.

Mary returns with more towels and kneels at Varina's feet and
rubs olive oil on her ankles.

VARINA

Mr. Benjamin, you certainly have a way with words.

JUDAH

Mrs. Davis, I am a lawyer . . . and today I am
my own client. I am trying to make a compelling
argument for your friendship. I think your husband
is a great man. We stand on the precipice of a great
new experiment. If we win we change the world.

VARINA

And the experiment is working?

JUDAH

I look at your husband as the modern day George Washington. This is our American revolution.

VARINA

I think my husband is destined for greatness.

JUDAH

We have been very fortunate . . . but this is very early on . . . we have taken the necessary steps of freeing ourselves from a government that didn't have our best interest at heart. The Southern states have united, we have the finest man working for our success . . . but we have not won the war . . . yet.

VARINA

I believe you and Jeff can do it.

JUDAH

The Battle of Bull Run was a hard fought victory. Now the world is watching us. We've been recognized by the Pope. France, Spain, and other European countries are starting to acknowledge our right for sovereignty. I'm here to ask the President to send an envoy to England, so that the Brits might join us in this war and fight with us.

VARINA

You think they will?

JUDAH

It could be very profitable for them. They import a lot of Southern goods. We will make it very appealing for them. It will be an investment in their future business dealings with us.

VARINA

My, my, my . . . Mr. Benjamin, I like the way your mind works. Remind me never to play chess with you.

JUDAH

Please Mrs. Davis, call me Judah. I love this new country we are building. I love the South. I admire, respect, and marvel at the great qualities your husband possesses.

VARINA

Please Judah, call me Varina.

JUDAH

We are at the dawn of a new age. Anything I can do to insure our place at the table where other nations dine . . . I will do.

VARINA

Judah, I am so glad we had this little talk. You have set my mind at ease . . . and reassured my heart. I can see why my husband values your counsel.

Mary replaces Varina's slippers on feet. Jefferson comes to the doorway.

JEFFERSON

Ah, Judah, there you are. Come let us plot the demise of some Yankee soldiers.

Jefferson exits. Judah kisses Varina's hand.

JUDAH

First Lady Varina Davis, I must leave . . . but I look forward to our next conversation.

VARINA

Judah, hopefully you will bring me news of a British ally.

JUDAH

Varina, may it come to pass that someday you dine with Queen Victoria.

He kisses her hand, then exits.

VARINA

Mary are you done?

MARY

Yes ma'am.

Varina drinks the rest of the green fairy.

VARINA

I wonder if Queen Victoria likes peach preserves.
I'm hungry. Think I'll have Sarah Mae make me a
sandwich with some of your famous tasty bread.

Varina exits. Mary gathers the towels.

Black Out.

Scene VII

Davis White House Office. Jefferson is sitting at his desk as Judah enters.

JEFFERSON

Judah, did you bring your notes for the meeting?

JUDAH

Yes, J. D. before we do that I would like to offer a proposition.

JEFFERSON

Proposition? What kind of proposition?

JUDAH

Strategy . . . but you must first let me finish with my thought. You must hear me out.

Mary enters and she starts polishing the furniture.

JEFFERSON

Judah, you underestimate your value you to me. I want to know how that devious mind of your works. Of course I will hear you out.

JUDAH

I want you to think about this before we present it to the rest of the cabinet.

JEFFERSON

Yes Judah.

Judah pulls out a cigar case from his jacket and he takes a cigar and offers one to Jefferson. Jefferson declines.

JEFFERSON

No thanks.

JUDAH

J.D. we should free our slaves.

JEFFERSON

Have you lost your mind?

JUDAH

We'll put them in the army.

JEFFERSON

No.

JUDAH

I asked you to hear me out.

JEFFERSON

Judah, why do you think we fight this war? Those Yankee devils want us to do just that. They are now using it as a battle cry to enlist more soldiers.

JUDAH

We need help to win this war. England would enter the war on our side if we but free our slaves.

JEFFERSON

Out of the question.

JUDAH

In Britain they have abolished slavery. It is the major sticking point of contention with any nation that might help us.

JEFFERSON

I don't care. I want my niggers.

JUDAH

If Queen Victoria sees that we have freed our slaves, we take away the moral issue Lincoln is counting on to rally his forces. Think of this rationally.

JEFFERSON

It is not a moral issue. It is economics pure and simple. Slaves are property. I am not being irrational, Judah.

JUDAH

Well, J. D. we could . . .

JEFFERSON

I can't have young white crackers fighting side by side with niggers.

JUDAH

Why not?

JEFFERSON

Because they don't own any slaves. They will see they are not part of our aristocracy.

JUDAH

You can convince them by using southern patriotism. You are our Washington, we need those black bodies shooting Yankees.

JEFFERSON

Judah, we need their labor in the fields, in the workshops and on the railroads, the canals, the highways. Listen my friend, we need those black bodies in the coal and iron mines. We can not give up their labor at this most important juncture of the war.

JUDAH

Point taken. I don't agree, but your point is taken.

JEFFERSON

Besides, Judah, do you think the rest of the cabinet will agree with that?

JUDAH

That is why I wanted you to lay the ground work now . . . for what is to come later. We are vastly outnumbered. Right now our enemy is inexperienced and they lack true leadership. Once they find a strong commander our battles will not be so easily won.

JEFFERSON

The bible says that niggers are the sons of 'Ham' . . . so it is out of the question. What is our next order of business?

JUDAH

I wanted to free our slaves before the yanks actually hit upon it themselves.

JEFFERSON

You think those Northern bigots will fight next to a nigger? Let us close this subject.

JUDAH

The yanks do not want free niggers running around their cities any more than we do . . . but they will do anything to win this war.

JEFFERSON

Next point of business.

JUDAH

J. D. one last thought . . . then I am finished.

JEFFERSON

What for God sakes? (He looks heavenward.) Knox . . . why do I have to endure this?

JUDAH

If the war keeps taking their men at some point they will enlist niggers to fight side by side with white men. Yankee white men.

JEFFERSON

I don't believe it. They are duplicitous. I used to listen to them talk about niggers in the halls of the Senate. They do what is politically expedient, nothing more, nothing less.

JUDAH

And so must we. J. D. free our slaves.

JEFFERSON

No. Yankees fighting with niggers. Not even they would do that. They are uncivilized beasts . . . but no one would want to fight side by side with a nigger. Who would put a gun in the hands of a nigger? For God sakes don't bring this up in our meeting. We will never get anything done. Don't worry about the mule going blind . . . just load the wagon.

JUDAH

I'd do it myself but I have enemies in that room.

JEFFERSON

As long as I am President your position is secure. Here is what I want to do next with our armies. I want to take Washington. We run that republican out of the white house . . . we will have both a moral and physical victory.

Judah looks at some maps on Jefferson's desk.

JUDAH
Let us look at our troops. That is a well guarded fortress.

JEFFERSON
If we work our way into their territory . . . start say with Baltimore, we could affect a blow that will devastate their spirit.

JUDAH
Good idea, J. D. General Johnston and General Beauregard had great success at Bull Run.

JEFFERSON
Beauregard is a pain in my ass.

JUDAH
I know that you and Gustave do not get along . . . but he is a savvy general.

JEFFERSON
We will lay options in front of Johnston. I would rather he led it . . . if he is of the opinion we are best served by using Beauregard, I will acquiesce.

JUDAH

Spoken like a true commander.

JEFFERSON

Come let us go. I don't want to be late for our meeting. Nothing worse than a roomful of fidgety peckerwoods.

JUDAH

Let me gather my notes.

JEFFERSON

Leave it. You know what you want to say.

Jefferson and Judah exit. Mary dusts the table where they were working. She is alone in Jefferson's office. She goes over his maps and some letters. She fakes dusting, then picks up another letter and reads it. Unknown to her, Old Robert enters the room. He watches her. She dusts some more then picks up another letter and reads it.

OLD ROBERT

I see what you was doin'.

MARY

You see me working?

OLD ROBERT

Naw. I seen what you was doing.

MARY

Old Robert, are you talking in riddles?

OLD ROBERT

No, little Mary . . . don't know no riddles. Just know
what I seen.

MARY

And just what did you think you saw?

OLD ROBERT

Know what I saw . . . saw you readin'.

MARY (laughs)

You know niggers can't read.

OLD ROBERT

Guess you ain't no nigger den, cause I saw you
readin'. Is you colored or just a Negro? You play
dumb . . . but you ain't. Been around a long time
little Mary . . . seen a whole lot of things. Good
things . . . bad things, beautiful things and some
down right evil things. I used to be young Robert,
don't ya know. I knows how to avoid trouble and I
knows how to multiply good times. You know how
I do that?

MARY

No, Old Robert, how do you do that?

OLD ROBERT

I look a person in dere eyes. A white man's eyes can't hold no secret without him telling you . . . it's a secret. Oh, I've seen 'em try to hide a secret, but I been around long enough to recognize a lie or see de truth . . . sitting right dere in dey eye. Know when a white man is scared and know when he's working himself up to beating a nigger's ass. It's all in dey eyes. If'n I take my shirt off, you ain't gonna find no scars on my back. Dat ain't no accident. I know de truth of what I see. I'm gonna ask you a question little Mary . . . if'n you value Old Robert as a friend, you gonna look me in my eyes and you gonna spread truth all over your words.

MARY

I value you Old Robert.

OLD ROBERT

We gon' see. Little Mary Bowser was you reading Master Jeff private papers?

MARY

(beat) Old Robert, I want you to come close and look me dead in my eyes.

Old Robert moves to Mary.

MARY

Old Robert make no mistake . . . I can read any word put in front of me and write it too if I have a mind to do so.

OLD ROBERT

(beat) I knew it. I knew it. Little Mary, little Mary, I got you. Yes, indeedy I got you . . . got a secret to tell you . . . I knows' my alphabet . . . all 26 letters. Recognize certain words too. Want to know more . . . can you help me? It ain't easy around here. Want to be able to read . . . 'fore I die.

MARY

You want a teacher?

OLD ROBERT

Has to be done in secret.

MARY

You want to write too?

OLD ROBERT

Lord ham mercy . . . ain't you a God send. If it ain't a bother?

MARY

One is just as dangerous as the other. If we gonna leap into the river, might as well go with both feet.

OLD ROBERT

Little Mary, you got gumption. Ain't seen that in a Nigger's eyes since John Love ran north.

MARY

Old Robert, you ain't exactly what white people think you are. Are you? You have disguised your contempt for this most peculiar institution in a jovial demeanor.

OLD ROBERT (laughs)

Love the sound of them words. Promise me you'll show me what dey look like.

MARY

I promise.

OLD ROBERT

Guess you know your secret safe with me.

MARY

It's why I told you the truth. Shylock is the name of a character in a play. He lends folks money.

OLD ROBERT

What's the name of the play?

MARY

Mercantile of Venice.

OLD ROBERT

Who wrote it?

MARY

Willis Shake—the—spear.

OLD ROBERT

I'll say dis for you . . . you a pretty smart nigger.

MARY

Some might say . . . I'm special.

OLD ROBERT

Mary answer me this. Why you want to read Massa Jeff's private papers?

MARY

Old Robert, You know how white folks feel about darkies reading. If I open a book, I'm sure to get caught. If I glance at a paper and practice what I see, easier not to get caught.

OLD ROBERT

Yes sir, this is a brand new day. Gonna use that trick myself when I'm ready.

Old Robert exits humming. Lights slowly fade.

In the darkness the voice of Varina.

VARINA

Old Robert what are you humming about?

OLD ROBERT

Nothin'.

Black Out.

Scene *VIII*

Davis White House State Room. Varina is sitting at a table writing a letter and sipping her green fairy. Jefferson enters.

JEFFERSON
Who are you writing to?

VARINA
Mary Chestnut.

JEFFERSON
Mary Chestnut? That's the woman got an ass like a forty dollar mule.

VARINA
Stop it, Jeff.

JEFFERSON
A fact is a fact. Your hair looks beautiful.

He touches, then strokes her hair, he kisses her on the forehead. She pats his hand.

JEFFERSON
Why you writing her?

VARINA

The lack of a social circle here . . . or the lack of my acceptance into a social circle here. Have you been using my stationary?

JEFFERSON

No . . . why?

VARINA

I'm sure I had more paper than I have.

JEFFERSON

Say hello to her husband. Haven't you been making friends here?

VARINA

Richmond is hard Jeff. I heard a rumor, they like calling me Queen Varina. These women seem to want to criticize you before they get to know you.

JEFFERSON

All of them?

VARINA

Well, Lizzy is a dear. She has been a great help and a blessing to me. I would more of the ladies were as open and kind as she.

JEFFERSON

She may be crazy but at least she has good taste in choosing her friends.

VARINA

And how are things progressing with the war? May a wife be of assistance to her husband? May the lady that is first in your life be the first to hear?

She sips from her glass. He reads the letter in his hand

JEFFERSON

I'll tell you Varina . . . General Johnston is really starting to become a pain. First it was Beauregard, now it looks as if he's poisoned the well and I'm getting resistance from Johnston. His animosity leaps off the Goddamn page. He acts as if I was never a soldier or knew anything about fighting on a battle field.

VARINA

Get rid of him. Demote him.

JEFFERSON

I can't do that he is too valuable.

VARINA

He knows that. Therefore he is being arrogant . . . Beauregard too. Promote Lee. You like him and he seems quite capable.

JEFFERSON

Robert E. Lee?

VARINA

Yes. That will give Johnston and Beauregard their comeuppance and it lets them know they can be replaced.

JEFFERSON

That is actually a good idea, Varina.

VARINA

Every once in a while a wife can rise to the occasion.

JEFFERSON

Yes you can.

He leans in and kisses her on the forehead. As he withdraws she grabs him around his neck and kisses him full on the mouth. They break.

JEFFERSON

Taste's like absinth.

VARINA

It comforts me. Oh Jeff. Some days I wish you were a dry goods clerk . . . then we could dine in peace on a mutton scrag at three and take an airing on Sunday in a little buggy with no back, drawn by a one-eyed horse at fifty cents an hour. Then Yankees or no Yankees we might abide here or there or anywhere.

JEFFERSON

Someday Varina you will have that, except I want a horse with two good eyes.

She laughs. They kiss again.

Black Out.

Scene IX

Davis White House Kitchen. It is night. Mary and Old Robert are sitting at a table. There are writing utensils on the table. Mary is pointing to some letters on a piece of paper.

OLD ROBERT

X. Y. Z.

MARY

You didn't miss a one. You know your alphabet.

OLD ROBERT

Told ya'.

MARY

Look at these five letters. Can you tell me what they are?

OLD ROBERT

A.E.I.O. Uhhh. Is dat a word?

MARY

No . . . but they are real important letters. They help make a word. Say it again.

OLD ROBERT

A.E.I.O. Uhhh.

MARY
That last letter is pronounced 'U'. Say that . . . 'U'.

Old Robert flirts with Mary as he says . . .

OLD ROBERT
'U'.

MARY
Good. Those letters are called vowels. Now, on this
piece of paper I want you to write those letters.

OLD ROBERT
Nice paper where'd you get it?

MARY
You want to learn to write or you want to open up a
stationary store?

He clumsily picks up the pencil and tries to write. Mary comes
back to the table and helps him hold the pencil. He continues
to flirt with Mary.

MARY
We are going to have to destroy that paper you know
that?

OLD ROBERT
Damn sho' do.

He continues to write.

OLD ROBERT

Can I ask you a question?

MARY

Don't worry . . . we'll do the rest of the letters later.
First I want you to understand what these letters do.

OLD ROBERT

Dat weren't my question.

MARY

Oh. Sorry.

OLD ROBERT

Miss Elizabeth give you a man?

Robert cannot see her eyes as she answers this question.

MARY (laughs)

I ain't married.

OLD ROBERT

Little Mary Bowser, if I was ten years younger . . .
you'd be mine. I'd have Miss Varina buy you for me.

MARY

Ten years?

OLD ROBERT

Okay, twenty years younger.

Mary gives him a look.

OLD ROBERT
Okay, okay, okay, thirty years. Black don't crack.

MARY
Thirty years younger? They should call you 'Not so
Old Robert'.

OLD ROBERT
Damn, can you tell how old I is? All right forty
years younger . . . and dat is all dat I am admitting
too . . . I would make sho' your master was good to
you. I'd make sho' you was fed with dey leftovers.

MARY
You got those kind of privileges?

OLD ROBERT
Little Mary, I knows how to handle white folks.
Look at my belly. I come by dat honest.

MARY
Oh, you come by that honestly?

OLD ROBERT
Dat comes from good eating. Dey like me . . . and
dey feed me. How does dis letter look?

She looks at the letter.

MARY

That's good. Don't stop. Keep going.

He writes another letter.

MARY

You was never married?

OLD ROBERT

Oh, I had me a beautiful wife when I were a young man . . . had her for fourteen years, den they sold her. She some place in Tennessee. We was in love. I sho' did love me some Lorraine Brown.

MARY

Lorraine?

OLD ROBERT

High yellow gal. She loved her some Robert Brown too . . . had four chillun. I was young den. Young and hot and full of devilment.

MARY

Where are your children now?

OLD ROBERT

Wished I knew. Sold. Some place in the South . . . though I think my youngest boy is up North. Boston. He might even be free by now. He was a smart one. Knew how to work dose white folks.

MARY

Like his daddy.

OLD ROBERT

Spittin' image, too. Amos Brown, yeah . . . he was my heart, don't ya know.

MARY

Amos Brown, of Boston.

OLD ROBERT

Maybe. Wish I could have seen them grow up. Ernestine, Olive, Sylvester and Amos . . . dose were mine. Lorraine sure knew how to make beautiful babies.

MARY

Those were yours?

OLD ROBERT

Hell, a gal as pretty as Lorraine . . . you think de master wasn't gonna give her some children? She had twelve. How's dis letter?

MARY

That's good, keep going.

OLD ROBERT

What is dis on top of de line?

MARY

That is a dot. The letter 'i.' Union win this war maybe some day you see your children. Go, north and find Amos.

OLD ROBERT

Little Girl, think it . . . don't say it.

MARY

They say Union win this war, we all be free.

OLD ROBERT

A little late for me don't you think? It ain't possible. Freedom? Dis dog is too old to learn that new trick.

MARY

Old Robert . . . look at yourself. Right now you learning how to write. and doing a damn good job.

She lifts up the paper and examines the letter 'i' he has written.

MARY

Maybe its time to rethink your situation.

OLD ROBERT

Oh Lordy, time to go.

MARY

Where you going?

OLD ROBERT

Need to do my favorite chore.

MARY

But you're not finished.

OLD ROBERT

Has to wait . . . dis is more important.

Lights go to half.

Scene X

Lights go up to half on Jeff Davis' White House Office: Old Robert stops and leans in the doorway. Lights fade out in kitchen as Mary examines Old Robert's writing. Lights up full in Jefferson's office as Old Robert enters.

OLD ROBERT

Is it time?

Jefferson is sitting at his desk going over some papers.

JEFFERSON

Yes, it's time.

Old Robert comes into the room.

OLD ROBERT

How was your day Massa Jeff?

He gets a decanter of whiskey and pours whiskey into a fine crystal glass.

JEFFERSON

Let us thank God for small rewards.

OLD ROBERT

Yes sur.

Old Robert hands Jefferson the drink.

JEFFERSON

Deo Vindice

OLD ROBERT

That's that dead language thing ain't it?

JEFFERSON

That's right Old Robert. Latin.

OLD ROBERT

I knew it was that or French. What it mean?

Old Robert gets a worn mug and pours a shot into that mug. He sits in a chair.

JEFFERSON

'God, Will Vindicate' . . . Think I'll make that our motto. Deo Vindice.

OLD ROBERT

So, we winning, huh?

JEFFERSON

Yes, Old Robert, we've been winning our battles. We won 'Bull Run'. Lincoln has just replaced General McDowell with General George McClellan. McCellan is a joke, that man is a martinet not a strategist. We put those Yankees in a tizzy.

OLD ROBERT
Massa Jeff, I heard Mr. Judah saying something about dat 'Bull Run'. . . . but don't know quite what it's all about?

JEFFERSON
Tell me, what did you hear?

OLD ROBERT
I allowed how some body's bull got out, and us and de Yankee's was trying to catch him and get him back in de pasture.

JEFFERSON (Laughs)
Old Robert, that is quite logical. Very good. That is not the case but I am impressed with your sense of logic.

OLD ROBERT
Is I close?

JEFFERSON
Bull Run is the name of the place where we fought the Yankees. It's in Manassass. We were not chasing a bull. We were shooting at each other.

OLD ROBERT
And we won?

JEFFERSON
Captured almost a thousand Yankee prisoners.

OLD ROBERT

Hot—Too—Mah—Dee No! Dat's a real whuppin'.
What you gwine do wid'em?

JEFFERSON

There is a warehouse here in Richmond. The Libby
Building.

OLD ROBERT

Den it's gwine be the Libby Prison?

JEFFERSON

Yes . . . and my generals gave me a little bonus.
Bragging rights to take to Lincoln.

OLD ROBERT

What yall braggin' about?

JEFFERSON

First . . . pour me a little more Kentucky Mash. Deo
Vindice. *Putting our hearts in God and in our own
firm hearts and strong arms we will vindicate the
right as best we may.*

Old Robert gets up and pours his master a little more whiskey.

OLD ROBERT

Twelve year old Kentuck taste good.

JEFFERSON

Yes it does . . . and it satisfies my soul.

OLD ROBERT
Massa Jeff, where did my Lorraine go?

JEFFERSON
Lorraine? Lorraine, Lorraine . . . oh yes, Lorraine.
Why do you ask?

OLD ROBERT
You say . . . 'satisfied my soul.' Dat little gal made
my soul satisfied. Just wonder if she safe . . . in dis
war. Wonder where she might be?

JEFFERSON
My Daddy, sold her to Forrest's Memphis slave pen,
but that was years ago. She could be anywhere.

OLD ROBERT
You think she safe?

JEFFERSON
No telling Old Robert. This is a war, and things are
starting to change.

OLD ROBERT
Why he sell her?

JEFFERSON
It was a business decision, Old Robert. Don't take it
personal. She stopped making babies . . . we needed
fertile girls and she passed her usefulness as a
breeder. It was time for a new investment.

OLD ROBERT

I shore did love dat gal.

JEFFERSON

She lost her value, Old Robert . . . had to be done.
I'm sure she ended up in some one's house and not
in the fields.

OLD ROBERT

You knows for certain?

JEFFERSON

Not sure . . . she could be anywhere. With this war
on . . . no telling where she's gone. That was so long
ago.

OLD ROBERT

Guess I lost dat gal to the mysteries of de unknown.

JEFFERSON

Don't fret, that milk is spilt. Let me tell you about
my bonus.

OLD ROBERT

Ready to hear it massa Jeff.

Old Robert goes to get a box cigars and first offers one to
Jefferson who declines then takes one himself and sits down.

JEFFERSON

A Congressman from New York, Alfred Ely came out of Washington to sit in his buggy and gloat. Thought we were going to lose the Bull Run Battle. Sat in his buggy eating fried chicken and corn bread, swilling down hooch. Sat there like he was in a theatre watching a play, ready to cheer on those blue coats.

OLD ROBERT

What's de bonus?

JEFFERSON

He's sitting in my new prison. That'll teach a Yankee to bet against us.

They laugh.

OLD ROBERT

No more fried chicken for dat Yankee. Sound to me like a good omen.

JEFFERSON

I'm not superstitious . . . but it is a good omen. I'll drink to that.

There is a knock at the door. Old Robert immediately gets up.

JEFFERSON

Who is it?

JUDAH (Off Stage)

Judah.

Judah enters the office and hands a letter to Jefferson.

JUDAH

I was told to give this to you right away.

Jefferson reads the letter and starts to pace as he reads.

JEFFERSON

Old Robert pour Judah a drink.

OLD ROBERT

Yes sur. Two fingers?

Old Robert gets a glass for Judah and pours him some whiskey. Jefferson is pacing and he is getting angry as he reads the letter in his hand.

JUDAH

Two fingers would be fine.

JEFFERSON

Son of a Bitch. Sons of bitches. Those goddamned Yankee, low life, conniving bastards.

Mary quietly slips in the room and starts to polish furniture.

JUDAH

What is it? What is the matter?

JEFFERSON

Read this.

He hands a letter to Judah.

JEFFERSON

God damn it Judah, read this. They're stealing my niggers.

JUDAH (He reads.)

Three slaves, Frank Baker, James Townsend, and Sheppard Mallory had been contracted by their masters to help construct defense batteries at Sewell's Point, for the confederacy. So . . . so what?

JEFFERSON

Keep reading.

JUDAH

They escaped at night and rowed a skiff to Old Point Comfort, where they sought asylum at Fort Monroe. The Yankees agreed to asylum?

JEFFERSON

That's outright stealing. Any runaway that gets to the union lines is now classified as contraband. The nerve of those bastards. We have an agreement . . . The Fugitive Slave Act. They have an obligation to return our slaves

JUDAH

No J. D. they don't.

JEFFERSON

What do you mean they don't?

JUDAH

The Fugitive Slave act started eleven years ago. We are now a foreign power. They had an obligation to the United States. We are no longer united. We seceded. This is very clever . . . very smart. Who did this?

JEFFERSON

You're saying those Yankee bastards can take my niggers? Is that what you're tellin' me? They can legally do that?

JUDAH

We are at war. New rules are made up every day to support each side.

Mary continues to dust around the room.

JEFFERSON

Those three runaways get to Fort Monroe and beg the Yankees to give them asylum . . . and those bastards do it! Then when we requested their return, sons of bitches started this contraband shit. That's legal?

JUDAH

General Butler . . . hmm . . . is a clever son of a bitch. You have to admit this is very smart, J. D. very smart.

JEFFERSON

I don't have to admit a god damn thing. Smart or not, I want my niggers back.

JUDAH

The only way we can do that is to take Fort Monroe. They are playing a hard fought game. Score one for the blue. It is time the grey came up with some counter move. Something that will upset Lincoln as much as he's upset you.

JEFFERSON

Damn right.

JUDAH

Let us ruminate on this situation and then come up with a viable counter attack. We must not let emotions dictate our actions.

JEFFERSON

Okay. Okay. What about our navy? Has the Merrimack been converted yet?

Judah checks his notes. Mary continues to dust.

JUDAH

Yes. It is now the CSS Virginia. It should be seaworthy by February.

JEFFERSON

Let's figure out a plan to slap those Yankees silly. Let them look to the land and we shall arrive by sea.

Judah starts writing notes on a piece of paper. Varina enters. She has a glass in her hand and takes a sip.

VARINA

There you are . . . Old Robert, I need you.

Old Robert crosses to the door.

VARINA

Gentlemen I need two more strong men. Can you I impose on you just for one minute of your time.

JEFFERSON

Hell no!

JUDAH

Certainly, Varina . . . come on Jeff we need a little calming down period.

JEFFERSON

Varina, this isn't gonna take all day is it? What are you drinking?

VARINA

The green fairy.

Jefferson takes the glass from Varina's hand and sets it on a table, then exits; leaving Mary alone in the office. Mary goes and gets a book and opens it and lays it on the table. She gets a pencil and paper from her apron and writes down some notes from the papers on Jefferson's desk. Her back is to the door. Varina returns. She cannot see that Mary is writing but she does see her hunched over the table.

VARINA

Mary what are you doing?

Mary hides the paper and pencil under her dust cloth.

MARY

Nothing.

VARINA

Clearly you were doing something. What was it?

MARY

Just dusting.

VARINA

No, you weren't Mary. I'm not a fool. You dusted this room yesterday. It's clean as a whistle. Now I want you to look me in the eye and tell me what you were doing. You know I can tell when some one is lying. I just look into their eyes and I can see it.

Now I am gonna ask you one more time . . . what
were you doing?

> MARY

Reading.

> VARINA

Reading? You can read?

> MARY

Yes ma'am. Been reading for about two years now.

> VARINA

Let me see what you were reading.

Mary hands Varina the open book.

> VARINA

Show me what you were reading.

On both of the pages of the open book are pictures.

> MARY

I been reading this here.

> VARINA

There are no words on this page, it's just a picture.

> MARY

That's what I was reading. The picture.

VARINA

You were reading the picture?

MARY

Yes ma'am.

VARINA

That is not called reading Mary. That is picture gazing. You were looking at the picture or gazing at the picture.

MARY

I thought that was reading.

VARINA

Oh God No!! No! No!

MARY

That's what this field hand told me, told me I was reading . . . .

VARINA

No! No! Oh, my water, Mary, call my husband, the baby is coming . . .

Varina grabs her stomach and collapses in a chair. Mary holds onto her. The "Battle Hymn of the Republic" begins to softly play.

MARY

I can't leave you.

VARINA

No Mary . . . quickly get my husband.

Mary crosses to the door and as she does she stuffs her handwritten note under her dress. Varina doesn't see this.

MARY

Massa Jeff, Massa Jeff . . . .

She runs out of the room. As the lights fade to black Varina clutches her stomach and screams. It is the scream of a mother giving birth. The "Battle Hymn of the Republic" continues to play.

Black Out.

End of ACT I

Act I

Left to right: Chrystee Pharris, Connie Ventress, Lou Beatty, Jr.
(Act I, Scene 2)

Left to right: Paul Messinger, Gordon Goodman (Act I, Scene 5)

Left to right: Anne Johnstonbrown, Chrystee Pharris, Connie Ventress (Act I, Scene 6)

Left to right: Anne Johnstonbrown and Gordon Goodman (Act I, Scene 8)

Act II

Left to right: Connie Ventress, Robert Pine (Act II, Scene 1)

Left to right: Chrystee Pharris, Paul Messinger, Gordon Goodman
(Act II, Scene 3)

Left to right: Chrystee Pharris, Lou Beatty, Jr. (Act II, Scene 5)

Casts

Left to right: Chrystee Pharris, Ted Lange, Anne Johnstonbrown, Gordon Goodman, Paul Messinger, Connie Ventress, Robert Pine. (Hollywood Hudson Theatre—Opening Night Cast)

Left to right: Robert Pine, Connie Ventress, Anne Johnstonbrown, Gordon Goodman, Chrystee Pharris, Lou Beatty, Jr., Paul Messinger (National Black Theatre Festival—Opening Night Cast)
Photos by Mary Lange

ACT II

Scene I

Van Lew Pantry. Four years later, Elizabeth and a Yankee journalist, Mr. Slydell are kissing. She breaks the kiss.

ELIZABETH

Kissing you is like brushing my lips against velvet. Tender. You have a way about you . . . don't you Mr. Slydell? Velvetize me again. (He kisses her again.) Oh, yes. Soft and tender . . . yet confident and assured . . . velvet. Not many men can blend those assets.

SLYDELL

You flatter me Miss Van Lew.

ELIZABETH

Young men are too eager. They rush the moment . . . overwhelmed by their passion. Satisfy the carnal. Damn the lady . . . ready or not here I come . . . but you Mr. Slydell, you understand the virtues of patience. You savor. You use tenderness as a means . . . to seduce my soul. (She kisses him) Spend the night.

SLYDELL

Miss Van Lew I am indeed honored and I thank you for extolling my limited virtues . . . I sometimes feel that women will play the innocent maiden and pretend they do not want, what they really do want . . . but you . . .

ELIZABETH

Spend the night.

SLYDELL

Does it show on my face?

ELIZABETH

Does what show?

SLYDELL

I am losing my resolve. Gettysburg has maimed my soul.

ELIZABETH

You are a journalist. You must write what is in your heart . . . the truth.

SLYDELL

I have something for you.

He reaches into his saddlebag. He has a small sack of flour. He gives it to Elizabeth.

ELIZABETH

Flour.

SLYDELL

So that you might make one of your delicious peach pies.

ELIZABETH

Generous as well as thoughtful . . . yet, I am incapable of satiating your palate. I thank you but I must return this to you.

SLYDELL

Pray tell what stops you from receiving my gift?

ELIZABETH

There is not enough flour here for half a dozen biscuits, let alone a Van Lew peach pie. This city has been devastated and fresh fruit is not a high priority value item. Plus I have asked you to spend the night twice to no avail. A woman with half a brain knows that when an invitation is extended and no response if forthcoming . . . consummation is highly unlikely.

SLYDELL

War has trumped free will. Men like myself must look to the future for the solace of female companionship.

ELIZABETH

Spend the night.

SLYDELL

I have another token.

He opens his saddlebag and produces a mason jar of peach preserves. He gives the jar to Elizabeth. He places the sack of flour on a small table.

ELIZABETH

Peach or apricot?

SLYDELL

Why peach of course. I can not pass the fruit and not think of you. A fresh ripe peach holds all the mysteries that I share with you. Delicate texture . . . you cannot squeeze it too hard or its body will bruise . . . the sweet natural juices that run off its body seduce my every thought.

ELIZABETH

Mr. Slydell you must tend my garden with those strong hands and prune my tree.

SLYDELL

My duty asks of me . . . obligations. I want to be your gardener . . . but I must journey to Gettysburg tonight.

ELIZABETH

Pray tell what obligation awaits you in Gettysburg?

SLYDELL

I must carry the information you entrust with me
to our contact . . . and President Lincoln is giving a
speech. They are marking the day of the great battle
on what is now hallowed ground.

Slydell leaves the sack of flour. Elizabeth turns to a shelf
of jars and finds a small package among the many jars of
herbs. Inside the package are cigars. She hands him the cigar
package.

ELIZABETH

The information that our friends seek is hidden
among these smokes.

SLYDELL

Will you share with me who is your inside man?

ELIZABETH

Someday.

SYLDELL

There will come a time when we can control
our priorities . . . but death is still at the door . . .
wanting to claim more lives. Good night, my fair
lady.

He starts to leave, she stops him.

ELIZABETH

I look to the day of peace. Appease me before you go, Mr. Slydell. Would you at least leave me with the tender feel of velvet?

They kiss again.

Black Out.

Scene II

Davis White House State Room. The room looks weathered. Things are falling apart. The war has taken its toll on the room. Mary is brushing Varnia's hair and holding Varina's baby. Elizabeth enters. She is carrying a basket.

ELIZABETH
Good morning, good morning, got you something for the new baby.

She takes a box out of her basket.

VARINA
Isn't that sweet. what is it a doll? . . . just what she needs. I had her playing with Maggie's toys. What is this?

Varina hold up a pocket watch with a pink ribbon attached.

ELIZABETH
A pocket watch.

VARINA
Trust me Lizzy . . . she is not old enough to tell time.

ELIZABETH

But someday she will be . . . and she will be way ahead of children her age.

VARINA

You are one of a kind.

ELIZABETH

Are you ready to have another one?

Varina places the watch on the table.

VARINA

I think my body has been ravaged enough. After that scare three years ago with Billy, I had to be real careful with this pregnancy.

ELIZABETH

No, absinth this time?

VARINA

Not one drop. I learned my lesson. Winnie is one healthy little girl. Mary, where is my mirror?

ELIZABETH

How is Billy doing?

VARINA

That boy is full of piss and vinegar. He is running me ragged. I thank you once again for Mary.

Sometimes I need her just to occupy him so I can get work done.

Mary stops brushing Varina's hair and goes to a table and gets an ornate hand mirror. She gives the mirror to Varina. Varina gazes at her face in the mirror.

ELIZABETH
I have another surprise for you.

VARINA
A surprise?

ELIZABETH
Varina, it's very special . . . and I only want to share it with you. I've got a lovely treat for us.

Elizabeth takes a clothe napkin which has something in it out of her basket. Varina looks in the mirror.

MARY
You look beautiful Miss Varina.

VARINA
Mary take Winnie to Alberta. It's time for her milk.

MARY
Yes, ma'am.

Mary and the baby leave. Elizabeth takes out a jar of peach jam.

ELIZABETH

You still using Alberta as a wet nurse?

VARINA

Lizzy, no one can suckle a child like that nigger. She must have something special in her milk. (looking in the mirror) Do you think the war has ravaged my face?

ELIZABETH

Absolutely not. Other than myself you are the most beautiful woman in Richmond.

VARINA

I see plates, is this treat something to eat?

ELIZABETH

What is the one thing that is getting harder and harder to find?

VARINA

Lizzy, everything is harder to find. Fresh fruit, bread, vegetables, you name it and Richmond doesn't have it. This war is killing us.

ELIZABETH

Well, I brought something to lighten your spirits. Unwrap this.

Varina unwraps the clothe napkin. Inside is a warm biscuit.

VARINA

Oh my God, Lizzy. How did you manage this? Flour is so scarce, everyone is using corn meal.

ELIZABETH

I know. Minerva Meredith got hold of some flour and she baked half a dozen biscuits. She gave me and some other ladies each a biscuit.

VARINA

You want to share half a biscuit?

ELIZABETH

You're my friend.

VARINA

It's half a biscuit Lizzy. You eat the whole thing.

Varina slides the biscuit to Elizabeth.

ELIZABETH

We're friends. We should share. Minerva is a great cook.

Elizabeth slides it back to Varina.

VARINA

That's crazy, I shouldn't really. As much as I want to . . . I shouldn't.

Varina slides it back to Elizabeth. Elizabeth cuts the biscuit in half and puts jam on her half.

ELIZABETH

Why?

VARINA

Isn't Minerva the one who led the bread riot?

ELIZABETH

No, that was Mary Jackson.

VARINA

And . . .

ELIZABETH

Want some peach preserves on your half?

VARINA

Minerva was the other woman. If Jefferson ever found out I was eating a biscuit baked by the hands of Minerva, he'd kill me.

ELIZABETH

Varina, I don't have a dog in this fight.

Elizabeth takes a bite.

ELIZABETH

Oh my God, this is delicious.

VARINA

Did you put jam on the other half?

ELIZABETH

No. Want me too?

VARINA

Well, if you did that . . . I would be forced not to let
it go to waste.

ELIZABETH

Well, in that case . . .

Elizabeth puts some jam on the other half of the biscuit. She
extends her hand with the biscuit. Varina starts to take it then
hesitates.

VARINA

Oh, you Satan . . . this has got to be our secret.

ELIZABETH

I won't tell a soul.

Varina starts to take the biscuit, pauses, then decides to take
it, she has a bite.

VARINA

Sweet baby Jesus that's good!

ELIZABETH

Told ya'.

VARINA

Secrets, I've got another secret. Can I trust you? Oh Hell, I can't tell you. I can't tell anybody.

ELIZABETH

Varina, you don't have to tell me. Just enjoy your biscuit.

VARINA

How is your herb garden?

ELIZABETH

Unattended. I need a gardener.

VARINA

You don't have someone to tend your garden?

ELIZABETH

The war has killed off or maimed any good chance I have of finding a decent gardener.

VARINA

I guess it has.

Varina picks up her mirror.

VARINA

I see more lines.

ELIZABETH

There was a time I didn't have to worry. I knew there would be someone to till my soil, and nurture and coax my garden . . . so I would bring forth radiant flowers.

VARINA

My face is so consumed by battlefields, I wonder if I'll ever have any more flowers.

ELIZABETH

Now I am not as interested in flowers as I am in having someone with good strong hands to till my soil. Slowly and methodically, someone who can . . .

Varina takes another bite of her biscuit.

VARINA

Hmmmm. This is a sin and I know it.

ELIZABETH

Why would President Davis be upset with you for enjoying this biscuit?

VARINA

Don't you remember what happened in the riot?

ELIZABETH

I remember how it started. The ladies went to Governor Letcher, asking for help, businesses were raising their prices and they couldn't buy food. They were starving, all they needed was a little help and he turned them down.

VARINA
Right, right . . . then all the women marched toward the capital and the Washington statue.

ELIZABETH
I wasn't there but I heard maybe five hundred women gathered as they marched.

VARINA
More like a thousand . . .

Varina takes another bite of her biscuit.

VARINA
As the size of the crowd grew . . . slap me silly, but this tastes good. I haven't had bread in six months, no nine months, wait . . . no, no, no, longer than that.

ELIZABETH
Everything is so hard to come bye. I need long feet and strong hands.

VARINA
Lizzy! Let me finish my story . . .

ELIZABETH
Okay, okay, okay, okay.

VARINA

A thousand women were marching down the street. Truth be told, I was kind of proud of them . . . until they started smashing windows and taking food supplies. That was shameful.

ELIZABETH

I know Varina, but they were starving . . . and that bastard Letcher wouldn't help.

VARINA

Nothing he could do. So they went to Mayor Mayo.

ELIZABETH

Mayor Mayo, he's as useful as a sixth toe.

VARINA

Oh, he's a horse's ass, alright. Jeff told me Mayo read some gobble de gook to the crowd and then told them to disperse.

ELIZABETH

Who's gonna listen to a man with a squeaky voice. He's a soprano looking for a baritone.

VARINA

That's when Jefferson stood up in the wagon asked for their attention and got it.

ELIZABETH

He's a wonderful speechifier.

VARINA (she stands)

"You say you are hungry and have no money; here this is all that I have." And he reached into his own pocket, took out what he had and flung his dollars and coins into the crowd.

ELIZABETH

And . . .

As Varina speaks she picks up the pocket watch.

VARINA

No one budged . . . except for some small children that scrambled for the money. Then he pulled his pocket watch out of his pocket and said; "If you do not disperse within five minutes, the order will be given for the militia to fire on you."

ELIZABETH

And they ran like jack rabbits.

VARINA

Jeff later had them arrested.

ELIZABETH

Who?

VARINA

Minerva and Mary . . . so you see I don't want him to find out about this.

ELIZABETH

Hell, I can't tell Minerva that I shared this with you . . . the woman whose husband put her in jail? Uh-uh, that would upset her. It's our secret.

VARINA

I've got another secret. A big one.

ELIZABETH

About Minerva?

VARINA

No Lizzy . . . about the war.

Varina gets her brush and brushes her hair as she speaks.

ELIZABETH

You gonna tell me?

VARINA

You promise not to tell anyone?

ELIZABETH

My word as a Southern lady and a patriot.

VARINA

There is a leak in Jefferson's cabinet.

ELIZABETH

A leak?

VARINA

Someone is sharing confidential information with the enemy.

ELIZABETH

A spy?

VARINA

Stephen Mallory and Robert Toombs think it's Judah . . . but I know they don't like him because he's a Jew.

ELIZABETH

What do you think?

VARINA

I don't think its Judah. I trust him with my life. I know he is one hundred percent behind Jeff.

ELIZABETH

Are you sure?

VARINA

Lizzy some of the ideas he's come up with to help us win this war are brilliant. He's a genius . . . and I don't mind saying that . . . Jew or not.

ELIZABETH

Could it be one of the other members of the cabinet?

Elizabeth packs her picnic basket.

VARINA

Personally I think its John Reagan.

ELIZABETH

What does Jefferson think?

VARINA

He's in a quandary. We've tried on several occasions
to catch the culprit to no avail.

ELIZABETH

You've got to use stronger glue. Make a note of that,
tell Jefferson . . . stronger glue. You'll catch him.

VARINA

Glue?

Elizabeth picks up the pocket watch and places it in the middle
of the table.

ELIZABETH

It's really very simple. You put the secret on a
table, then put puddles of glue near the secret. The
poltroon perpetrator steps in the glue and now you
know who he is. Just check everybody's shoes.
Strong glue lasts a long time.

VARINA

Yes, of course Lizzy . . . stronger glue. You still
visiting the prison?

ELIZABETH

Yes and Chimborazo hospital. Not enough help to go around. What ever I can do to ease the suffering. Yankee or Reb they're just young boys that need caring for.

Elizabeth rises to leave.

VARINA

Lizzy, you are a good Christian woman. Can I keep the peach jam?

As Elizabeth hands her the jar.

ELIZABETH

Varina, I must confess to you, I know who the spy is?

VARINA

You do?

ELIZABETH

Of course I do . . . it's the Jew.

There is a knock on the door and as it opens, Judah enters.

JUDAH

The president is meeting with Robert Toombs. Mind if I join you for a few minutes?

ELIZABETH
Speak of the devil and up pops you know who? Mr. Benjamin, I am just on my way out to do my civic duty.

JUDAH
Ahh, Miss Elizabeth Van Lew, please give my regards to your lovely mother.

ELIZABETH
I shall Mr. Benjamin, I certainly shall. I don't think my garden's going to produce any flowers, but that doesn't mean I don't want someone trying. Stronger glue Varina, stronger glue.

Elizabeth exits. Judah sits down near Varina.

JUDAH
Is she all right?

VARINA
Who can say?

JUDAH
And how are you today, Varina?

VARINA
Fair to midlin'.

JUDAH
Anything I can do?

VARINA

Oh, Judah, Judah . . . . oh, I guess I'm fine. How is your wife?

JUDAH

At this point . . . I don't know. I haven't been able to receive any letters from Natalie . . . nor send any of mine to her.

VARINA

Miss her?

JUDAH

I miss my daughter Ninette.

VARINA

Will they ever come back to the states?

JUDAH

In her heart of hearts Natalie thinks she is a Parisian. I would like Ninette to see the South . . . but the way things are going who knows if that will ever be possible?

VARINA

Are you lonely?

JUDAH

I am alone . . . but not lonely. The war occupies so much of my mind I don't have time to indulge in loneliness.

VARINA

Indulge? Indulge . . . Judah . . . sometimes I get so lonely. Jefferson is right here in this house, but he might as well be in Paris with your wife. Everything consumes him. Everything except family.

JUDAH

I understand. When this war is over Varina . . . you will get your husband back.

VARINA

I had to tie him down just to get him to stop long enough to give me Winnie. He completely ignores the children. I look at him and see his mind is off somewhere thinking of schemes and tactical strategies. I miss his touch. How do you modify your life without your wife?

JUDAH

Varina, I will be honest. I'm afraid I love my wife more than she loves me. I have had to structure my living in a way that benefits my career, more than my family.

VARINAS

Do you miss her touch?

JUDAH

Deeply.

VARINA

What sustains you Judah?

JUDAH

Before this war it was knowing . . . every summer
would be shared with her and Ninette in Paris.

VARINA

And now?

JUDAH

Why do you ask?

He kneels to her.

VARINA

I need something to sustain me. Win or lose, I need
to devise a way of keeping my sanity.

Varina leans in to kiss Judah, but resists.

VARINA

I need to fight for my marriage.

JUDAH

He loves you.

VARINA

That man in the other room is not my husband. He
is a President. He is building a nation. He is not the
man I married.

JUDAH

Leadership is a tiresome burden.

Judah stands. As Varina speaks, she picks up her mirror.

VARINA

I would like to see the man I married occasionally.
I would like to feel the warmth of his touch . . . the
tenderness of his spirit. I want him to gaze upon my
face and smile.

Judah takes the mirror from Varina.

JUDAH

Varina . . . in my mind, I have rooms. In each room
I place things I need and things I love. Right now,
the room that holds my family . . . my wife, my
daughter, that room is locked. They are shut away.
I try not to think on them. Someday I will unlock
that door and let the sunlight illuminate that room.
So that even the darkest corner gleams like freshly
minted gold.

VARINA

You will illuminate that room.

JUDAH

But for now I must work in a room that stimulates
my mind and re-enforces the work that must be
done now.

VARINA

Judah, you are such a comfort to me.

JUDAH

My only wish is for your happiness.

VARINA

Thank you.

She extends her hand. (a beat) He takes her hand in his . . .
they look into each other's eyes . . . Judah leans in to kiss
her. She does not resist. Old Robert enters and interrupts the
moment.

OLD ROBERT

Sir, Massa Jeff is ready to see you now.

JUDAH

Thank you.

Judah exits. Old Robert hums as he exits. Varina is alone. She
picks up her mirror and looks at her face. Her finger traces a
new line she has discovered.

The lights fade. Black Out.

Scene III

Davis White House Office. Jefferson is sitting at his desk. Judah enters. He hands Jefferson a letter.

JEFFERSON

What's this?

JUDAH

An endorsement, for freeing the slaves.

JEFFERSON

From whom?

Mary enters with a tray with a teapot, cups, and cookies.

JUDAH

Your favorite General. Robert E. Lee. He agrees with me.

JEFFERSON

Damn you Judah.

JUDAH

J.D. we have no choice. It has to be done.

JEFFERSON

If we take them for public service, the government must pay their owners for them. Each regiment of a thousand slaves would cost the government, two hundred thousand dollars.

JUDAH

Gettysburg devastated us. We're still recovering. If we don't do this you might as well surrender.

JEFFERSON

We would have to sell them at the end of the war or give them their liberty . . . and that my friend is an odious affair, at the very least.

JUDAH

We have the money.

JEFFERSON

I can't believe Lee approves of this.

JUDAH

He wants men. He's not a fool. You can't fight a war without soldiers. The English refuse to help us. We've run out of options. Who cares if confederate soldiers are white or black.

JEFFERSON

I care.

Mary hands a cup and saucer to Jefferson.

JUDAH

We are not on the battlefield. As long as a nigger can point a gun at a Yankee and pull the trigger, we live to fight another day. J. D., come down off the cross, we need the wood.

JEFFERSON

But will they pull the trigger?

JUDAH

And that my friend is why we must offer them their freedom. Those Northern niggers have been pulling the trigger against us. We are offering our niggers their legal freedom. No contraband, no counterfeit Emancipation Proclamation. Believe me, offer them freedom and they will take it and shoot a Yankee quicker then a drunken sergeant at a Quaker meeting.

Mary hands a cup and saucer to Judah.

JEFFERSON

That son of a bitch Lincoln, he had no authority to free our slaves . . . we are a sovereign country.

JUDAH

It's all perception J.D. No one listens to the rules.

JEFFERSON

Those coons listened and ran . . . they ran to daddy Lincoln . . . it's illegal.

Mary pours tea into Jefferson's cup.

JUDAH

That's why we must legally free our slaves.

JEFFERSON

I free our slaves . . . and all hell is gonna break loose.

JUDAH

J. D. we've been living in hell these past four years. This war has devastated our country. What are we really giving up?

JEFFERSON

Everything! Our way of life . . . the social fabric of Southern society . . . without cheap labor . . . our whole economy would fall apart.

JUDAH

You don't do this . . . we lose the war. Even Lee can see that. If we get captured, they will try us for treason.

JEFFERSON

They can't do that. We have legal rights to do what we did.

Mary pours tea into Judah's cup.

JUDAH

J. D. The winner makes the rules. You know that.
How much leniency do you think they will extend
to you?

JEFFERSON

This just gripes my ass. Niggers in our army.

Mary serves a plate of cookies to Jefferson.

JUDAH

I just want to win and I don't care who is responsible
for our victory. If we lose you can always protest
this in a Yankee court. History will note your rights
to secede have been abused . . . but you will be
swinging at the end of a rope and no one will care
what circumstances transpired for you to end that
way.

Judah and Jefferson drink tea.

JUDAH

Give them their freedom . . . but don't give them our
rights.

JEFFERSON

What does that mean?

JUDAH

J.D. I'm a lawyer. You let those niggers fight for
their freedom Okay? Okay, they can become

soldiers . . . after the war, if they live, they've earned their freedom . . . but we will write laws. New laws . . . laws that dictate what a nigger can do and what they cannot do.

Mary serves a plate of cookies to Judah.

JEFFERSON
But what keeps them from living in the North?

JUDAH
J. D. we have to be subtle. These laws can't look like they are against a nigger, it has to look as if it is for a nigger. We develop a code. A way of reading the law, so that a sheriff or a judge can use it in a proper way. They will be free, but they will never be our equal.

JEFFERSON
Free but not equal . . . done. Okay, we enlist colored soldiers.

JUDAH
Do you think you can sell it to the others?

JEFFERSON
I'll explain it . . . and those peckerwoods will buy it. What have you found out regarding the leak?

JUDAH

J.D. It has to be one of the cabinet members. I just haven't deduced which one. I've narrowed it down to two . . . but all the pieces don't fit.

JEFFERSON

Which two?

JUDAH

Robert Toombs has plenty of motive . . . since I took his place as secretary of state.

JEFFERSON

It's not Toombs. That Georgian's too arrogant. And besides he's been on the battlefield for the last two years. Who else?

JUDAH

John Reagan has had plenty of chances to pass information . . . but it just doesn't make sense.

JEFFERSON

I think its Mallory. He keeps talking about resigning.

JUDAH

But he's been very effective with our navy.

JEFFERSON

God damn it, who is this bastard? He's dug in like an Alabama tick.

JUDAH

Whoever it is foiled us once more. Our plan to have Captain T. Henry Hines free our Confederate prisoners from camp Douglas was defeated. There is treachery about us and for the life of me I am confounded.

JEFFERSON

And what of New York?

JUDAH

Our spies were able to set fire to a dozen hotels and we did some damage to P. T. Barnum's Museum.

JEFFERSON

Keep at it! I want to do to that city what Sherman did to Atlanta. Whoever this traitor is . . . he'll slip up and I want to catch him and skin him like a cornered badger in a skunks holler.

Mary drops a book.

JUDAH

We've got to lay a sound trap for him. Something that will smoke him out . . . even a blind hog finds the acorn.

There is a knock at the door. Old Robert sticks his head in the door.

OLD ROBERT

Is it time?

JEFFERSON

Yes, it's time. Thank you, Judah. I will have something for you tomorrow. Give this note to Wilkes-Booth.

Hands a letter to Judah. He takes it.

JUDAH

I will set up the meeting with the other cabinet members for tomorrow morning, nine am.

Judah exits. Mary gets the crystal glass and pours whiskey into it and give it to Old Robert. Old Robert hands the glass to Jefferson.

OLD ROBERT

How was your day Massa Jeff?

JEFFERSON

I think God has turned against us Old Robert . . . but I'll be damned if I will let us be ruled by some corrupt, arrogant, Northerners . . . using slavery as an excuse to glorify control over my country. I've been a good master to you haven't I?

OLD ROBERT

You been my only master. Far as I can remember I been owned by de Davis family.

JEFFERSON

We've been living this way for two hundred years. Yankees want to take away . . . the best part of living.

Mary hands Old Robert his mug.

OLD ROBERT

Take what away?

Mary pours whiskey into Old Robert's mug.

JEFFERSON

Those Yankee's think I'm licked. I ain't licked. This war is over when I say it's over.

OLD ROBERT

Looks like Yankees are getting close to Richmond. What 'cha gwine do, dey take Richmond?

JEFFERSON

Old Robert one must always have an alternative plan. If the Yankees take Richmond, I will travel to Texas, unite the regiments that can get there, and join forces with Kirby Smith.

OLD ROBERT

Start a whole new army.

JEFFERSON

Got enough gold, plenty of silver. I'm a soldier, I'll die fighting. They want my gun? They will have to pry it from my cold dead hand.

OLD ROBERT

Massa Jeff, don't want to see you end up in Arlington.

Mary offers Jefferson a cigar. He declines.

JEFFERSON

Arlington, another example of Northern arrogance.

OLD ROBERT

Not sure I understand what you mean.

Mary offers Old Robert a cigar. He accepts.

JEFFERSON

Old Robert you know that Robert E. Lee's plantation was Arlington?

OLD ROBERT

Yes, Massa Jeff. I know Jim Parke, Massa Robert E. Lee's nigger . . . know the union asked him to dig the first two graves for the Yankees that died in Battle.

JEFFERSON

Buried those damn Yankees on Lee's plantation. Turned the grounds of Arlington into a cemetery for Union soldiers. A slap in the face to Lee, just because he chose to fight for me rather than fight for them. Even when we win this war, Lee can never go home.

OLD ROBERT

They say Jim Parke buried some Union colored soldiers at Arlington too.

JEFFERSON

That's outrageous.

OLD ROBERT

Guess they all alike once they in the ground.

JEFFERSON

The true beauty of war is things can change at any moment . . . Mary pour me a little more Kentucky mash.

Mary pours Jefferson another glass of whiskey.

OLD ROBERT

Twelve year old Kentuck taste good.

JEFFERSON

I got plans for Lincoln. He's not getting away with this sacrilege.

Black Out.

Scene IV

Van Lew House, Pantry. Mary meets Elizabeth in the herb
closet. Mary drops the slave lingo and speaks as an educated
woman.

MARY

Betty, these cigars are from Jeff Davis's private
collection. The information is inside. I also found
some troop movement. Lee is moving his men to
Petersburg.

ELIZABETH

He won't be able to hold that. General Grant will
march right into this city. He'll take Richmond,
move on to Petersburg and cut Lee off.

MARY

Their only choice will be to retreat to Appomattox.

ELIZABETH

I've got to get this information to General Grant.

MARY

To the point Betty . . . old man Davis wants to
enlist colored soldiers. If they serve they will be
emancipated . . . it's ludicrous.

ELIZABETH

Davis has agreed to use colored soldiers? Never thought I'd live to see this day.

MARY

They enslave an entire race of people and in order to sustain their corrupt, demented view of life . . . they give the very people they loathe a chance to kill for them.

ELIZABETH

Desperation my dear . . . but it's too little . . . too late.

MARY

You think so?

ELIZABETH

Mary, this war is over. It's been over . . . Jeff Davis just doesn't know it.

MARY

Judah Benjamin thinks they can revive their cause with colored troops.

ELIZABETH

Judah Benjamin better think of an escape route. It's just a matter of weeks, if not days. The confederacy is ending and there is no way to stop it. We won.

A male figure enters and stands in the shadows observing the two women.

MARY

We did . . . didn't we?

ELIZABETH

Mary, you are a patriot. You gave up your life of freedom so that others may gain theirs. You returned here for an honorable cause.

MARY

That college you enrolled me in, paid us big dividends in this little escapade. (slips back into slave talk) "Once you taste freedom, Miss Elizabeth you want everybody to sip from that bowl."

ELIZABETH

I told your husband that you would be returning tonight. I don't want you to stay any longer than necessary. Your work is done.

MARY

No Betty . . . I'm not finished. I have one more final act to carry out before I escape.

ELIZABETH

Mary, I feel they are getting too close to the truth. I don't want them to discover your involvement. We got lucky when Varina was pregnant with Billy . . . and we were able to take advantage of the situation.

But since the birth of Winnie, you've had too many close calls. Get out now . . . they are too aware . . . it doesn't feel good.

MARY

Betty, that is an evil house. You read some of the machinations they plotted in his office. Before I go, I have something to do. Something I must do. I will meet you tomorrow.

ELIZABETH

What do you plan on doing?

MARY

Carpe Noctem.

ELIZABETH

Seize the night? No whatever it is it's too risky.

MARY

Something poetic. The kind of thing Dante would relish had he sat on the third ring of hell and gazed at the impending doom of an enemy.

ELIZABETH

Okay . . . but I want you to meet me tomorrow night at Tom McNiven's house.

MARY

I just need one night.

ELIZABETH

I will arrange transport for you north. Which city do
you want to end up in?

MARY

I want to go back to Philadelphia.

ELIZABETH

Where shall I tell you husband to meet you?

MARY

Ask Wilson to meet me in front of the Liberty
Bell . . . at noon on Wednesday. It's been a long
time. The man is a saint, Betty. The United States
of America owes him. I plan to make his four year
abstinence a memorable reunion.

ELIZABETH

Done. Wednesday, noon. You be careful. I don't
want you getting hurt, when we are this close to
achieving our goals. Mary Bowser, you are real
special to me.

MARY (slave lingo)

Miss Elizabeth . . . don't you know, I know that.

Mary exits. Elizabeth crosses upstage to the figure. The man
comes out of the shadows and it is Mr. Slydell.

SLYDELL

So that's your inside man. Very clever, Miss Van
Lew.

ELIZABETH

Why Mr. Slydell, that woman has done more to keep
the union together than any Yankee gun could ever
do.

Slydell kisses her hand and starts to leave. Elizabeth holds
onto his hand, smiles and pulls him back into the room.
Slydell follows her into her house.

Black Out.

Scene V

Davis White House Kitchen. Old Robert is sitting on a stool at the kitchen table, reading a book. Mary enters.

MARY
Look at chu . . . reading.

OLD ROBERT
Little Mary, I thank you for opening dis door.

MARY
My pleasure Old Robert.

OLD ROBERT
I still got to be careful . . . don't think it's a good idea for Master Jeff to know my new skills.

Old Robert shows her a piece of paper on which he has written.

MARY
Good penmanship, too. Not bad for an old dog.

OLD ROBERT
Just might write myself a pass and go north, don't cha know.

MARY
North . . . ain't you the one.

OLD ROBERT

Probably won't have to. Dis war is coming to an end and I am gonna be free and clear. Think I'll visit Boston.

MARY

Boston.

OLD ROBERT

Little Mary, I got a great expectation.

MARY (laughs)

You sure do if you thinking of going to Boston.

OLD ROBERT

Reading about dis here young man, in dis book . . . name of Pip. He had a great expectation.

Mary picks up the book and reads the cover, *Great Expectations* by Charles Dickens.

MARY

Charles Dickens. He's famous don't cha know.

OLD ROBERT

All I know is . . . I likes his writing. Now, dat I can read . . . I think I might be able to find my son, Amos. He's my heart, don't cha know. I'll start in Boston and work my way down.

MARY

If you find him . . . what will you say?

OLD ROBERT

Nothin'. First two days I'm just gonna look at him. Look at de curve of his face. De shape of his hands, see if he got calluses from work or if he used his brain and was able to make a life without breaking his back. Gonna see if he got fat or if he's strong and lean. Either way, won't matter, cause I get to sit in de room with my boy. Let him know . . . I'm his daddy. He ain't no white man's son. He's my son . . . and I will thank God he let me live for dis here moment.

MARY

That's good.

OLD ROBERT

Next two days . . . it will be just him talking' to me. I want him to squeeze his lifetime into two days. Tell me everything dat happened to him. Who he married? If he got kids? Can he cook? Did he fight in dis here war?

MARY

That's good.

OLD ROBERT

Now the next two days it will be my turn . . . I'm gonna talk fast so I get everything in. Let him know how I survived dis war. Tell him about some young

Nigger gal dat thinks she's special. Tell him how little Mary taught his daddy to read and write.

MARY

That's very good. What happens after that?

OLD ROBERT

Why Mary Bowser . . . don't you know dat will be the seventh day and dat's the day I'm gonna rest.

MARY (laughs)

Why of course Old Robert I should have guessed that.

OLD ROBERT

Maybe eat me a big ol' pot of black eyed peas for luck, with ham hocks dat fall off the bone. What are you gonna do after de war is over?

MARY

Don't know. I have to figure out something special for myself.

OLD ROBERT

Nothing ordinary, huh?

MARY

Why Old Robert . . . you know I'm a special nigger. Someday you gonna realize that. I got to find something extra special for myself.

OLD ROBERT

If you really are special . . . won't be too hard to do.

Mary picks up the pencil and starts to hand it to Old Robert as she speaks.

MARY

This war be over soon . . . and the world is gonna change for a colored person.

Black Out.

Scene VI

Davis White House Office. Jefferson is stuffing important papers into a carpetbag. Judah enters.

JUDAH

J. D. where's your family?

JEFFERSON

Train depot. What are your escape plans?

JUDAH

Florida Coast. It's easier to get to than Canada.

JEFFERSON

Oh, Judah, the South is my heart.

JUDAH

We can't stay in the South. There will be Yankee's everywhere. Our cities will be occupied with Union forces. We've got to get to Europe.

JEFFERSON

I'm going to Georgia. There are all kinds of small towns, little villages . . . Danville is no bigger than a gnat's ass.

JUDAH

No, no, no, you can't stay in Georgia. They'll find you, arrest you and hang you.

JEFFERSON

Judah, the South is my home. I love this land . . . I'm not leaving.

JUDAH

J. D. . . . that South you love is gone. Cities have been devastated. The Yankees are on their way to invade this city. Lee has already left for Petersburg. We sit here, unguarded.

JEFFERSON

So, your plan is Florida?

JUDAH

I've got a cousin in Ellenton . . . then I am leaving America . . . gonna try and get to Europe.

JEFFERSON

Judah, you would leave this land?

JUDAH

J. D. look at what the land has become.

JEFFERSON

Judah, we convene with the rest of the cabinet in Abbeville, then decide. We could go underground. Lick our wounds. We wait for time to give us a

chance to regroup. Reorganize . . . and we can come
back stronger than ever.

JUDAH

Have you forgotten this souvenir?

He picks up a cigar case from Jefferson's desk.

JEFFERSON

Ulric Dahlgren's cigar case. So What?

JUDAH

That was just one year ago and he got very close.

JEFFERSON

We caught him.

JUDAH

We were blessed with a lucky day. He could have
assassinated you. If we hadn't found his orders in this
cigar case . . . we have no idea how much damage he
could have inflicted. There are spies everywhere. At
this moment, who can you really trust?

JEFFERSON

I trust you.

JUDAH

Our cabinet doesn't. I'm not an idiot. I know what's
going on. I see it in their eyes. Ready to blame our
failures on The Jew.

JEFFERSON
We've got enough gold to . . . .

JUDAH
It's over Mr. President. We tried and we failed.

Varina brings Mary into Jefferson's office.

VARINA
Jefferson, I can't believe this. Look at her.

MARY
I'm innocent master Jeff.

JEFFERSON
What? Varina, why aren't you at the train depot?

VARINA
No you're not, you hussy.

JEFFERSON
Varina, the train leaves in less than twenty minutes.
I want you and the children on that train!

VARINA
I'm staying.

JEFFERSON
I want you to go. I need to know that you are safe in
Charlotte. Judah, is Harrison here?

JUDAH

Think he is waiting out front in the wagon. I'll check.

Judah exits.

VARINA

I am averse to flight. Let me stand by your side.

JEFFERSON

No! The children need you . . . and I need to know that you are safe.

VARINA

What about this bitch? I caught her . . . caught her red handed.

JEFFERSON

Mary, what did you do?

MARY

Nothing.

VARINA

I caught her . . . caught her downstairs.

JEFFERSON

Downstairs?

VARINA

She had straw and was starting a fire.

MARY

I'm innocent. Master Jeff, I'm innocent.

Varina slaps Mary. She falls to the floor.

VARINA

I'm not a liar. She had a torch . . . used my silk
blouse wrapped around a stick as a torch. She was
lighting the house on fire.

JEFFERSON

Is the fire out?

VARINA

I caught it in time. Jesse and Sarah Mae were able to
extinguish it.

MARY

It was an accident.

VARINA

She could have hurt our babies.

JEFFERSON

Mary Bowser . . . what do you have to say for
yourself?

MARY

It was an accident.

VARINA

You had a torch!

JEFFERSON

I don't have time for this. Yankee's getting close.

Judah returns and sticks his head in the door.

JUDAH

Harrison's waiting. She's got to get to the depot.

VARINA

I'm giving this gal thirty lashes.

JEFFERSON

Varina, I'll handle this. Judah get me Old Robert.

Judah exits.

JEFFERSON

Remember what I told you. I'm going south to Danville.

VARINA

I want to be with you.

JEFFERSON

I do not expect to survive . . . . you and the children must live to carry on the Davis name. Where's the gun I gave you?

VARINA

I packed it away in my trunk.

He goes to his desk and gets a gun.

JEFFERSON

I want you to be armed at all times. Remember how I taught you to use this?

VARINA

Yes.

JEFFERSON

You can at least, if reduced to the last extremity force your assailants to kill you . . . but I charge you solemnly to leave when you hear the enemy approaching; and if you cannot remain undisturbed in our country, make for the Florida Coast and take a ship to a foreign country.

VARINA

I love you Jeff.

He kisses her.

JEFFERSON

I love you Knox.

VARINA

Knox?

JEFFERSON

What?

VARINA

Jefferson, you called me Knox.

JEFFERSON

I did not.

VARINA

Yes. Plain and clear.

Judah enters with Old Robert.

JUDAH

Varina, you have to leave that train won't wait forever.

Varina points her gun at Mary's head and cocks the gun.

VARINA

Let me shoot this nigger.

JEFFERSON

Varina, I said I would handle it. Old Robert . . .

OLD ROBERT

Yes Sur, Massa Jeff.

JEFFERSON

Take this child to the kitchen and tie her up.

OLD ROBERT
Yes suh.

Old Robert exits with Mary.

JEFFERSON
I will be there shortly. Varina, you know I love you.

VARINA
Evade those Yankees, Jefferson.

Jefferson and Varina kiss.

JEFFERSON
I will meet you. Judah, get my family to the train depot.

Judah exits with Varina. Jefferson returns to his desk and continues stuffing the carpetbag with important papers.

Black Out.

Scene VII

The Davis Kitchen. Old Robert is tying Mary up.

OLD ROBERT
Little girl what did you do? You done raised de hackles on Miss Varina something fierce.

MARY
Old Robert, you got to let me go.

OLD ROBERT
Cain't do dat. Massa Jeff gave me an order.

MARY
It's over. Time is up. The Confederacy is dead, they just don't know it. There is not going to be a second country in America. There is only the United States of America. It is a new day for black folks Old Robert. You ain't that old dog no more, you getting educated. You don't have to obey orders anymore, you ain't a slave. You are a man. Yes, you are black . . . but you are now a man. Let me go. Show these white folks you part of this new world that's coming. Show me you don't have to bow down to a white man. Show yourself what's really in your soul. Let me go, Old Robert, so I can live my life as a free woman. So I can bring babies into this new world . . . free of their past . . . and ready to build a

new future. Let me go Old Robert and fill your heart with justice.

He looks at her for a beat, then unties her.

OLD ROBERT
Looks like my back gwine get some well earned scars.

She starts to leave, but stops and goes back and kisses him on the cheek.

MARY
Come with me. You don't need to endure no beating on my account. Come with me Old Robert. Be free with me.

OLD ROBERT
You think dis old dog can handle being free?

MARY
Can you read and write?

OLD ROBERT
Little Mary I believe you done made a point. I think dis endeavor can be fortified wid immediate action.

MARY
Damn right.

OLD ROBERT

You go on. Got to get a few things, I'll catch up.

MARY

Meet me at Tom McNivens House.

She looks him in his eyes, then runs off. Old Robert goes to get a gunny sack. He goes around the kitchen putting food into the sack. Jefferson enters.

JEFFERSON

Where 's the girl?

OLD ROBERT

Gone.

JEFFERSON

I gave you an order.

OLD ROBERT

Yes suh. I know.

Jefferson looks at Old Robert and crosses to him. Jefferson is defeated. It takes a beat for him to realize that his world has changed.

JEFFERSON

You too?

OLD ROBERT

I ain't no dog. I'm a man. My time has come.

JEFFERSON

I guess it is a new day.

OLD ROBERT

Yes suh, it is. I'm walking into a new life, Mr. Jeff.

JEFFERSON

A new life.

OLD ROBERT

Mr. Jeff, gwine be free and gwine find my son.

JEFFERSON

What do you think those Yankee's are going to do to my wife and children if they catch them? You think they are going to be good to them as I was to you? I need someone to look after them.

JEFFERSON

Old Robert I need you.

OLD ROBERT

You don't want me to be free.

JEFFERSON

What I want is . . . a favor. I don't have any rights to ask this favor . . . but I am going ask it, Old Robert. If the Northerners see you with my wife and children they will be less capable of doing harm. If I die, I have no one to see to their needs. If I get captured . . . I will be hung. I need to know there is some one to look after the Davis family.

OLD ROBERT

Mister Jeff . . . I gots a chance to live my life in a new way, Gots a chance for dese old eyes to see some joy.

JEFFERSON

I need you Old Robert. Will you consider one last request from me, before you take your freedom?

Old Robert looks at Jefferson. They stare at each other.

Black Out.

Scene IX

1865, Barren Room. Varina is under town arrest. She is living in Savannah, Georgia. Old Robert is with her. She is being interviewed by the Yankee journalist, Mr. Slydell. She sips from a glass. There is a bottle of absinthe next to the glass.

VARINA

What have I done that I am a prisoner at large? My family in a strange place . . . I am surrounded by detectives who report my every visitor?

SLYDELL

Surely you must find Savannah preferable to the things that are happening in Richmond.

VARINA

Answer this . . . why am I kept in a garrisoned town? Bereft of home, friends, husband and the means of support?

SLYDELL

You are a traitor to the United States of America.

She takes a sip of absinthe from her glass.

VARINA

Mr. Slydell, I detect a certain nastiness in your tone. I have answered all of your questions . . . yet I have noticed that you have gotten progressively hostile as you continue to question me. Is not a journalist supposed to remain, objective?

SLYDELL

And who is that man standing behind you?

VARINA

That's my nigger. Surely you will allow me to have one nigger?

SLYDELL

We Yankees look on the Negroes as people.

VARINA

So do I. Tell that to Horace Greely and your New York Tribune readers. All my other niggers have fled North . . . thank God for the loyalty of at least one family nigger.

SLYDELL

What's your name, sir?

VARINA

Robert Brown.

SLYDELL

Robert Brown you know that you are free now?

VARINA

Mr. Slydell, would you take my last nigger?

SLYDELL

I'm not taking him. I'm just informing him he now has a choice. He has rights. What do you say Mr. Robert Brown? Are you going to exercise your rights?

OLD ROBERT

Sir, I have examined my options and I have elected to stand by my mistress in her hour of peril.

Varina is amazed at his use of the English language.

VARINA

Thank you Old Robert. I hope you will print those words for your Tribune readers.

SLYDELL

This is an interview to get your side on the record, Mrs. Davis. I am not taking a political position. I would like to remind you that there are those who want to hang Jeff Davis.

VARINA

Hang him? I predict they will never 'try' my husband. They hold him in jail at this very moment and they have not brought any charges against him.

SYLDELL

They will bring charges against him and his entire confederate cabinet. They've already apprehended most of them.

VARINA

Did they capture Judah P. Benjamin?

SLYDELL

He escaped to Europe.

VARINA

Paris?

SLYDELL

No, London. Turns out he has British citizenship.

VARINA

Ah, yes he was born in Saint Croix.

SLYDELL

He may be practicing law in London . . . but they will get him back.

VARINA

No they won't.

SLYDELL

Why do you say that?

VARINA

That Jew is smarter than you.

SLYDELL

Speaking of smarter than you . . . one of the reasons for your husband's downfall was the union spy Mary Bowser.

VARINA

Who?

SLYDELL

You had a slave working for you . . . Mary Bowser. She was a spy for the Union army.

She takes a sip from her glass.

VARINA

Sir, I think you are mistaken. I do not know a Mary Bowser. Nor was there any nigger I own spying on me, my husband or my family. Ain't that right Old Robert?

OLD ROBERT

Yes 'um.

SLYDELL

You know Elizabeth Van Lew, don't you?

VARINA

Yes I do.

SLYDELL

She has stated that she let you use her slave, Mary Bowser. Both ladies as it turns out were working as spies for the union.

VARINA (beat)

Mr. Slydell, I don't know any slave named Mary and as far as Elizabeth is concern everyone in Richmond can tell you . . . she is batty as a loon.

SLYDELL

They say your husband wore a dress to disguise himself and evade capture.

VARINA

Why Mr. Slydell, you are not half the man my husband is. Go to Fortress Monroe, go. Look into his eyes and ask yourself are those the eyes of a man afraid of capture. No sir. You'll see . . . those are the eyes of a man unafraid to face his destiny. You will see eyes that shine like freshly minted gold.

SLYDELL

You seem to still love him.

VARINA

Are you married sir?

SLYDELL

Yes I am.

VARINA

Then don't ask stupid questions.

SLYDELL

One final question . . . in 1845 you married Jefferson. I understand that before you started your honeymoon, he took you to Natchez, Mississippi to the grave of his former wife . . . Sarah Taylor.

VARINA

Knox.

SLYDELL

Yes, Knox. If he loved you as much as you say he loved you . . . what was the purpose of visiting his first wife's grave? Are you jealous of the ghost of his first wife?

She looks at Mr. Slydell, then takes her glass and reflects for a moment, she drains the glass.

VARINA

Mr. Slydell, you ever have a brush with greatness? And I don't mean as a journalist. Would you recognize greatness if it stood before you? I know who my husband is and from the moment I met him I knew the aura of greatness sat on his shoulders. I was the lucky one. I was lucky that whatever he saw in me he felt compelled to make it a part of his life. I want to share every waking moment with Jefferson Davis. I will not stop until I have achieved that. I write letters everyday to friends, enemies, and powerful people. My husband does not deserve this imprisonment. Every Southern soul that lives and breathes knows the greatness of Jeff Davis. What woman knows what I have known or has felt what I have felt? Martha Washington is the only woman that comes to mind. She watched her husband create a nation. A Virginian, I might add. I watched my husband create a nation . . . but before that baby could barely breathe . . . Yanks killed it. As nations I think we could have lived together . . . but now we will never know will we? Am I jealous of a ghost? No sir, she got a few months. I am getting a lifetime and I am securing the name of Davis for future generations.

SLYDELL
Thank you, Mrs. Davis. I think I got a clear picture. Thank you for taking the time to let me interview you.

VARINA
Mr. Slydell . . . you be sure to print what I said. Every word of it.

SLYDELL
Verbatim, ma'am. Verbatim.

VARINA
Mr. Slydell, I know you think the war is over . . .

SLYDELL

The Union won Mrs. Davis. I know you don't like hearing that but . . . it's over.

Mr. Slydell starts to leave.

VARINA

My dear boy, you will never capture the Southern heart.

SLYDELL

Mrs. Davis, what you detect in my voice is the anguish that this nation has suffered over the lives that were lost in preserving this Union. What you hear in my voice is the outrage I feel over the assassination of our President. I look at you and I see a woman who has been pampered and catered to her whole life, who ignores the welfare of other human beings, because of the color of their skin.

You use the words of God and being a good Christian woman to further the world you want for yourself, not furthering the world for the good of all. You parse out biblical phrases to suit your needs, but I can find no humanity in your heart for your fellow Christians. Deo Vindice, God will vindicate? You started a civil war . . . an incredibly devastating war. Sons were pitted against fathers, brothers against brothers mothers against daughters and friends against neighbors . . . for what purpose? So, that you could maintain a dying lifestyle? The

South started a war for the independence of your own private fortunes. You used Southern pride to lure young, innocent, poor Southern souls into a war for your southern elite. So you could make money on the backs of the less fortunate. So your morally corrupt husbands could continue to do business that tarnished the name of America.

Mrs. Davis, I saw more death and carnage in these last four years and I know it will haunt me for the rest of my life . . . and the enemy was my brothers and sisters. I'm glad you lost this war. Whether you like it or not . . . America is changing . . . whether you like it or not . . . we have become a stronger nation . . . . and whether you like it or not the death of Lincoln is not going to slow down this progress one bit. Mrs. Varina Davis, former first lady of the Confederacy, whether you like it or not . . . this is now a nation with liberty and justice for all. I want to emphasize . . . for all. Good night Mr. Brown, good night Mrs. Davis . . . may God have mercy on your soul.

Mr. Slydell exits.

VARINA

Old Robert would you give me another taste of the green fairy?

He pours more absinth into her glass, adds water, a bit of sugar and stirs it with a spoon.

The lights go to half.

Spotlight up on a writing desk Stage Right. Elizabeth is writing a letter to Mary. She lifts up the paper to read what she has written.

ELIZABETH
Dear Mary, I miss you. Things here in Richmond have not progressed as I had hoped . . . but I am sure time will eventually solve all problems. I am amazed at the cruelty one human being can inflict on another.

Spotlight on a writing desk Stage Left. A light comes up on Mary sitting at a desk she is reading Elizabeth's letter.

ELIZABETH/MARY
There are Northerners streaming into Richmond taking advantage of the plight of our city and our citizens.

Lights go down on Elizabeth as her voice fades into silence.

MARY
Since Lincoln's assassination, things are not as safe for me as I had hoped. I think I did us both a great disservice by letting people know of our patriotic contributions to the union. Now that the cat is out of the bag as to our involvement in the war as spies, it is no longer safe for you or I as it once was. My advice to you is to disappear. I'm sure Lincoln

would not have allowed all the corruption that our new President Johnson seems to let flourish. He is incompetent. I am ashamed and embarrassed that he is my President. Looking to a brighter future . . . Sincerely, Elizabeth.

Mary is sitting at the desk begins to write a letter to Elizabeth.

MARY
Dear Betty, wonderful news, I am pregnant.

Lights up on Elizabeth at her writing desk reading Mary's letter.

MARY/ELIZABETH
Finally, time for a family. I am looking forward to a healthy, strong baby.

ELIZABETH
No absinthe for this girl. Wilson and I have been thinking about moving to Boston. A perfect place for us to disappear. It is a big city and there are lots of Negroes there.

Lights fade on Mary as Elizabeth continues to read.

ELIZABETH
To insure that we stay anonymous, we are changing our name. I also want to see if I can find Old Robert's son, Amos. I'd like him to know what kind of a father he has. Wilson thinks he can find work as a leather craftsman. He is a freemason and there

is a Prince Hall Lodge located in Boston. There
is a school for blacks there called, The Phillips
School . . . Maybe I can get a job teaching spelling
or Shakespeare? You and I know that dreams do
come true. Look what has happened to our country.
All my best, Mary.
PS. Burn this letter.

Lights go to half. Lights come up full on Old Robert and
Varina. Old Robert hands a glass to Varina.

VARINA

Thank you Old Robert

Varins takes a sip, then she gets up from her chair.

VARINA

Where is my mirror?

She crosses the room then stops.

VARINA

Mary Bowser a union spy. It was not the Jew, it was
the nigger.

Varina exits. Music: America the Beautiful, Ray Charles
version plays. Lights do a slow fade on Old Robert standing
alone, lights come up to half as the figures of Elizabeth and
Mary are standing in the shadows.

Mary rises and picks up a loaf of bread.

RAY CHARLES (Voice Over, sings)
Oh, beautiful for spacious skies, for amber waves of
grain . . .

MARY
I ain't no ordinary Nigger Old Robert,

Mary crosses the stage to Elizabeth and hands her the bread.

RAY CHARLES (sings)
For purple mountains majesty . . .

Elizabeth takes a note out of the bread.

MARY
I'm a special Nigger . . .

RAY CHARLES (sings)
Above the fruited plans . . .

Elizabeth and Mary read the note.

MARY
and someday you are gonna realize that.

Lights go to black on Elizabeth and Mary.

RAY CHARLES (sings)
America, America . . .

Pin spot on Old Robert, he smiles . . . then laughs.

RAY CHARLES (sings)
God done shed his grace on thee . . .

Black Out.

END OF PLAY

Bibliography

Ballard, Michael B. *A Long Shadow.* Athens: The University of Georgia Press, 1997.

Berkin, Carol. *Civil War Wives.* New York: Alfred A. Knopf, 2009.

Boaz, Thomas M. *Libby Prison & Beyond.* Shippensburg: Burd Street Press, 1999.

Carretta, Vincent. *Unchained Voices.* Kentucky: The University Press of Kentucky, 1996.

Davis, Kenneth C. *Don't Know Much About the Civil War.* New York: Prennial, 1996.

Dray, Philip. *Capital Men.* Boston: Mariner Books, 2008.

Evans, Eli N. *The Lonely Days Were Sundays.* Jackson: University Press of Mississippi, 1993.

Foner, Eric. *Forever Free.* New York: Alfred A. Knopf, 2005.

Foote, Shelby.*The Civil War.* New York: Random House,1958.

Garrison, Webb. *Amazing Women of the Civil War.* Nashville:Thomas Nelson, 1999.

Goodheat, Adam. *1861 The Civil War Awakening.* New York: Alfred A. Knopf, 2011.

Hall, Jasper Newton. *At Death's Door.* Huntington: Blue Acorn Press, 2010.

Holzer, Harold, & Symonds, Craig L. *The New York Times Complete Civil War, 1861-1864.*

New York: Black Dog & Leventhal, 2010.

Martin, David G. *Gettysburg July 1.* Pennsylvania: Combined Books, 1996.

Mauro, Charles V. *A Southern Spy in Northern Virginia.* Charleston: The History Press, 2009.

Meacham, Jon. *American Lion.* New York: Random House, 2008.

Meade, Robert Douthat. *Judah P. Benjamin, Confederate Stateman.* Baton Rouge: Louisana State University Press, 2001.

O'Brien, Cormac. *Secret Lives of the Civil War.* Philadelphia: Quirk Books, 2007.

Pollard, Edward A. *Life of Jefferson Davis.* Philadelphia: National Publishing Company, 1869.

Rasmussen, Daniel. *American Uprising.* New York: Harper Collins Publisher, 2011.

Swanson, James L. *Bloody Crimes.* New York:. Harper Perennial, 2010.

Stampp, Kenneth M. *The Peculiar Institution.* New York: Vintage Books, 1956.

Tate, Allen. *Jefferson Davis: His Rise and Fall.* New York: Balch & Co., 1929.

Thomas, Emery M. *Confederate Nation 1861-1865.* New York: Harper Perennial, 2011.

Trammell, Jack. *The Richmond Slave Trade.* Charleston: The History Press, 2012.

Varon, Elizabeth R. *Southern Lady, Yankee Spy.* Oxford: Oxford University Press, 2003.

Winkler, Donald H. *Stealing Secrets.* Naperville: Cumberland House, 2010.